Davidson

1996

1598

A Year of Pageantry
In Late Renaissance Ferrara

medieval & renaissance texts & studies

VOLUME 71

Renaissance Triumphs and Magnificences
New Series • Volume 4
General Editor
Margaret M. McGowan

1598

A Year of Pageantry
In Late Renaissance Ferrara

by

Bonner Mitchell

Medieval & Renaissance texts & studies
Binghamton, New York
1990

A generous grant from the Graduate School and Office of
Research of the University of Missouri – Columbia
has assisted in meeting the publication costs of this volume.

Library of Congress Cataloging-in-Publication Data

1598, a year of pageantry in Late Renaissance Ferrara / with an
  introduction and notes by Bonner Mitchell.
     p. cm. – (Medieval & Renaissance texts & studies ; v. 71)
  Includes bibliographical references.
  ISBN 0-86698-080-6
  1. Processions – Italy – Ferrara – History – 16th century.
2. Pageants – Italy – Ferrara – History – 16th century.   3. Visits of
state – Italy – Ferrara – History – 16th century.   4. Papal visits – Italy –
Ferrara.   5. Renaissance – Italy – Ferrara.   6. Ferrara (Italy) – Social life
and customs.   I. Mitchell, Bonner.   II. Title: Year of pageantry in
Late Renaissance Ferrara.   III. Series.
GT5030.A15   1990
394'.4 – dc20   89-13154
                                                                           CIP

This book is made to last.
It is set in Goudy text, smythe-sewn,
and printed on acid-free paper
to library specifications.

Printed in the United States of America

Contents

Introduction

Contents

Facsimiles

Engravings

Preface and Acknowledgments

This volume differs from earlier ones in "Renaissance Triumphs and Magnificences" by dealing with a series of festive manifestations that stretched over a period of eleven months, rather than with one event, like a triumphal entry, or a short sequence of events related to a single occasion, such as a royal visit. The Ferrarese triumphs and ceremonies of 1598 are, however, united in that they all result from a decisive turn in the history of the duchy, namely, its devolution from the Este family to the Church, and an ensuing long visit from Pope Clement VIII. The festive events of the year constitute a brilliant episode of civic pageantry in a city whose political importance was, paradoxically, about to suffer a decline.

These events include six grand entries into the city, a royal marriage ceremony performed by the pope, and several other entries or processions of a less elaborate character. The five narrative accounts reproduced in this volume describe the six grand entries and the marriage ceremony, with accompanying entertainments. In my own narrative, entitled "The Pageantry of 1598," I have given some account also of several lesser occasions.

The *feste* of 1598 are distinguished from most earlier ones in Italy, France, and England by the amount of descriptive material published, or otherwise recorded, at the time. For four events—the entries of the cardinal, the pope, the duke of Parma, and the queen of Spain—more than one formal *livret* was printed. There is also some description of all events in the manuscript diaries of Ferrarese citizens or officials in the papal party. Because the *livrets* were written to inform the public (as well as to flatter the actors of the ceremonies), they are in general the most informative sources; but some additional information may be found in the diaries, which also have the advantage of containing short accounts of some lesser occasions. For the principal events, I have chosen in every case to reproduce the *livret* that contains the most first-hand information. My analyses of each event and its *apparati* have, however, also made use of other *livrets* and the diaries. Bibliographical descriptions of all the *livrets* and other sources, both manuscript and printed, may be found in the special Bibliography at the end of the Introduction.

The relative abundance of narrative records for the 1598 events is, unfortunately, not matched in the area of graphic illustration. None of the *livrets* includes engravings of the *apparati* constructed in the streets for the entries, although such engravings were no longer uncommon by the end of the sixteenth century. Nor, to my knowledge, have any unpublished drawings survived. On the other hand, two of the processions are illustrated, one of them in considerable detail. Antonio Tempesta's large, separately printed engraving of the papal procession, and the rather similar engravings of the same scene published with Angelo Rocca's Latin treatise both came out within a year of the event and are clearly based on fresh eyewitness reports, whether or not the artists themselves had been present. The case is different for three engravings of events during the queen of Spain's visit that appeared fourteen years later in a book commemorating funeral ceremonies for her in Florence. These drawings too, however, are in agreement with the written accounts, and must have been done after some consultation of them.

Reproduction of Tempesta's whole engraving, 396 cm x 590 cm, would not have been practical for this edition. If the large print had been reduced to one page, its details would have been too small to distinguish; and a number of separate pages would have been necessary to show all segments of the procession in proper scale. I have chosen to reproduce only the segment showing the first part of the papal party as it is about to pass through the decorated city gate. From the engravings of Rocca's treatise, I have included the one depicting the progress of the Holy Sacrament on the way from Rome to Ferrara, and another showing the central part of the papal procession into the city, with the Holy Sacrament, the body of cardinals, and the pope on his *sedia gestatoria*. Of three relevant engravings from the queen's funeral book, two are reproduced: that showing the entry of part of the royal party into the city, and another depicting a moment in the ceremony of the queen's proxy marriage to King Philip.

I have tried to direct the Introduction to an audience of general Renaissance scholars. Much knowledge about major Italian figures, events, and literary works of the period is assumed, but I have thought it right to bring together in organized form a considerable amount of detailed and scattered information that is not familiar to the average Renaissance scholar, even Italian ones, and that cannot readily be found elsewhere. The account of events leading to the devolution and to the departure of Cesare d'Este is based upon several longer studies and makes no claim to originality. The narration and analysis of the actual celebrations during 1598, based as they are upon all the published *livrets* and several manuscript diaries, constitute, however, a fuller sustained account than has been available heretofore. The survey of the festival *livret* in the Renaissance is also fresh and derives mainly from personal research.

In the various narratives that are derived principally from secondary, scholarly sources, I have undertaken to indicate the most important of these sources at the beginning, or at least in short order. Information from them is not further identified, but any additional, differing sources are pointed out. The great mass of the information in "The Pageantry of 1598" is taken from the printed *livrets* reproduced in this volume. I have not always specifically credited these primary sources, but have been careful to credit any different ones—generally other *livrets* or manuscript diaries—for certain details.

To complete the context in which the 1598 entries took place, I have provided succinct summaries both of earlier occasions of pageantry in Ferrara, and of the triumphal progresses from Rome and Austria that immediately preceded the Ferrarese receptions of the pope and queen. Because bibliography for Renaissance *feste* is still hard to come by, I have cited *livrets* or other contemporary sources for a number of events mentioned only briefly in the text of the Introduction, as well as for those treated more fully. At the end of bibliographic citations for sixteenth-century publications, I have indicated between brackets at least one library in which the work can be found.

I wish to thank the British Library for permission to reproduce in facsimile four of the festival accounts: the departure of Cesare d'Este and entry of Cardinal Aldobrandino; the entry of Pope Clement; the entries of the Venetian ambassadors and the duke of Mantua; and the entry of the queen of Spain. The Biblioteca Nazionale Centrale of

Florence has courteously allowed reproduction of the remaining *livret*, that recounting the entry of the duke of Parma.

The British Museum, Department of Prints and Drawings, has kindly allowed reproduction of a segment from Antonio Tempesta's engraving of the papal entry, while the Rare Book and Manuscript Library of Columbia University has given permission to reproduce two engravings from its copy of Angelo Rocca's *De Sacrosancto Christi Corpore*. I am grateful to the director of the Moreniana collection of the Biblioteca Riccardiana-Moreniana, Florence, for being allowed to reproduce engravings by Jacques Callot and Raffaello Sciaminossi from its copy of Giovanni Altoviti's 1612 funeral book *Essequie della Sacra, Cattolica e Real Maestà di Margherita d'Austria*.

Thanks are due as well for courtesies shown me in all of the libraries cited in the notes and bibliography, and particularly in those where the major part of the research was done: the Ariostea of Ferrara, the Estense of Modena, the Biblioteca Nazionale Centrale and the Riccardiana-Moreniana of Florence, the Bibliothèque Nationale of Paris, and the British Library, London. I wish also to thank Mr. Mario Lanfranchi, of Parma and London, a private connoisseur and collector of Renaissance festival material, for having permitted me to examine the catalogue of his collection and for having made available to me the Banordini account of Pope Clement's entry, of whose existence I had been completely unaware.

Abbreviations Used
in the Notes and Bibliography

Libraries and Archives

A.S.Fe.	Archivio di Stato, Ferrara
A.S.M.	Archivio di Stato, Modena
Ang.	Biblioteca Angelica, Rome
Arch.	Biblioteca del Archiginnasio, Bologna
Ariostea	Biblioteca Ariostea, Ferrara
Arsenal	Bibliothèque de l'Arsenal, Paris
BLL	British Library, London
BNCF	Biblioteca Nazionale Centrale, Florence
BNCR	Biblioteca Nazionale Centrale, Rome
BNP	Bibliothèque Nationale, Paris
Columbia	Butler Library, Columbia University, New York
Estense	Biblioteca Estense, Modena
Genoa	Biblioteca Universitaria, Genoa
Kansas	Spencer Library, University of Kansas, Lawrence
Lucca	Biblioteca Governativa, Lucca
Moren.	Moreniana Collection of the Biblioteca Riccardiana—Moreniana, Florence
Pavia	Biblioteca Universitaria, Pavia
Val.	Biblioteca Vallicelliana, Rome
Vat.	Biblioteca Apostolica Vaticana, Rome

Works

Faustini	Agostino Faustini's separately paginated continuation in the *Libro delle historie ferraresi del Sig. Gasparo Sardi* ... (Ferrara: Giuseppe Gironi, 1646).

Guarini, *Diario* I	Marc'Antonio Guarini's MS *Diario . . . di Ferrara* [*da*] *l'anno M.D.L.XX sino a . . . M.D.XXXXVIII*, further described in Bibliography.
Guarini, *Diario* II	His MS *Diario . . . di Ferrara principiando per . . . M.D.XXXXVIII*, further described in Bibliography.
Mucantius, *Diarium*	Giovan Paolo Mocante's MS *Diariorum . . . Tomus Quartus: De Itinere Clementis VIII . . . Rebusque Gestis . . . per Totum Annum M.D.IIC*, further described in Bibliography.
Pastor	Ludwig Pastor's *History of the Popes from the Close of the Middle Ages*, ed. Frederick Ignatius Antrobus and Ralph Francis Kerr (London: Kegan Paul, Trench, Trübner & Co., 1891–1954), 40 vols.
Rodi, *Annali* IV	Bound volume 4 of Filippo Rodi's MS *Annali di Ferrara*, containing the Second Part of the Fourth Book and all of the Fifth Book, further described in Bibliography.
RIS	*Rerum Italicarum Scriptores*, original eighteenth-century ed., Lodovico Muratori, new revised editions with various editors (Città di Castello: S. Lapi; then Bologna: Zanichelli, 1900–).

Introduction

The Festival Livret in the Italian Renaissance

Before the invention of printing, and for long afterward, official accounts of events of pageantry were often drawn up by hand to be preserved in court records, or to be sent to important personages in other cities. These manuscripts could be elegant works of art when, as happened occasionally, they were illustrated with colored miniatures.[1] There were also numerous unofficial handwritten accounts prepared by diplomats or commercial agents for governments and employers at home.[2] While the tone of official accounts is, of course, celebratory, that of the *avvisi*, or reports, varies according to the relation of the writer's home government or employers to the state in which the civic celebrations have taken place. Reporters to the Venetian *signoria* may, for example, write with sympathy of ceremonies in states allied to the republic, but differently of those at the courts of the republic's enemies. In general, however, the authors aim primarily at informing, rather than at persuading. With the exception of some high-level diplomats, most are anonymous, rather modest employees.

Printed festival accounts during the cinquecento owe something both to the tradition of the elegant manuscript *livret* and to that of the private, more or less confidential *avviso*. At the extremes one finds elaborate quasi-official *livrets*, on the one hand, and short free-lance *reportages*, on the other. The latter, called *avvisi* like their manuscript counterparts, become much more numerous after mid-century.

The earliest separately printed festival account of which I am aware describes celebrations for a princely marriage, that of the lord of Pesaro, Costanzo Sforza, to Camilla d'Aragona in 1475.[3] The tone is celebratory, and there is a good deal of occasional verse, but this very early *livret* also contains much information, from a report of the bride's arrival in the city to the description of a pageant and banquet. The anonymous author was almost certainly in the service of the ruling family.

The earliest published account I have seen of a properly triumphal event in Italy was published in France and is, as it happens, a falsified report:

> *Sensuyt lentree et couronnement du Roy nostre sire en sa ville de Napples le xxii. jour de fevrier mil. CCCC. iiii xx. et xiiii.* N.p.: n.d., but doubtless spring of 1495. [BNP]

In fact, no Neapolitan coronation of Charles VIII occurred on the date mentioned, and the entry was much less grand than alleged. Four years later there appeared a more reliable Latin report of the triumphal entry of Louis XII into Milan.[4] With his text in Latin, the author was not aiming at a large audience, although if the report appeared in Milan itself he may have been thinking of educated readers in the French expeditionary forces as well as of Italians.

The first Italian printed *livret* of the new century was, to my knowledge, an account of the Siennese celebration of the feast of the Assumption of the Virgin (August 15) in 1506.[5] Since the Virgin was patron of the city, celebration of this holiday had some civic content, analogous to that for Saint John's Day in Florence, or St. Mark's in Venice. The first properly triumphal event to inspire a formal, separately printed account in the cinquecento was apparently the coronation and *possesso* parade of Pope Leo X in 1513.[6] Like many later festival accounts in the sixteenth century, this one takes the form of a private letter from an observer to a patron. The author, Gian Giacomo Penna, is a Florentine physician residing in Rome, and he writes to the new pope's sister, Contessina de' Medici, back in Florence. This was of course in part a literary conceit, but the lady must at least have given her permission for the publication, and she may even have commissioned it. The author may also have received something from the printer. Despite his respectful attitude toward the Medici family, Penna did not write as a servile courtier. He is one of the rare authors of festival *livrets* to show a sense of humor, notably in contrasting his own lowly situation as a jostled spectator with the exalted places of precedence assigned to the dignitaries.

In the early decades festival accounts were sometimes written in verse, forming a sort of hybrid of journalism and occasional poetry. Several months before reporting upon Pope Leo's *possesso*, Penna had composed a versified description of a Roman carnival parade whose *apparati* honored Pope Julius II. Although that description is now known only from a manuscript,[7] it may well have appeared as a printed plaquette, like a number of other Roman carnival accounts later in the century. In the fall of that same festive year of 1513, the Capitoline ceremonies and entertainments for the granting of Roman citizenship to Pope Leo's brother and nephew gave rise to three printed verse accounts, as well as to several systematic manuscript descriptions in prose.[8]

Courtier poets continued thereafter to compose and to publish a great deal of occasional verse to congratulate high personages at the moment of triumphal entries, coronations, princely marriages and births (or to console them at the time of funerals), but such compositions were less often designed to describe and inform as well as to celebrate. Festival *livrets* came to be written nearly always in prose, although celebratory verses were sometimes included at the end of the accounts.

Very few *livrets* in the first half of the century contained woodcuts, apart from coats of arms on their title pages. It was, however, natural that authors should think eventually of providing illustrations of the triumphal decorations in the streets they described in the text. The earliest such illustrations to have appeared in an Italian *livret* are, so far as I know, four showing arches erected for the triumphal entry of Charles V into Milan in 1541.[9] These woodcuts are quite simple and reproduce few architectural details. In the late cinquecento, and especially in the following century, illustrations of *apparati* became much more common and much more detailed. Sometimes the blocks were carved in advance of the festive event by, or with the advice of, the designer of the constructions, so that publication would not be delayed. (Verbal descriptions of *apparati* were also sometimes prepared in advance for the same reason.)

The form of the private letter, with an observer writing to a friend or patron in another city, continued to be common for *livrets* but was more often a transparent literary convention, scarcely different from the practice of simply dedicating a work to a patron. The last decades of the century saw also the appearance of a less formal sort of *livret* written by a new sort of author. While the earlier writers had been men on the spot who seized the occasion to please a patron and win a bit of literary renown, some of the new ones were men in printing shops who put together reports from what we would call correspondents. These forerunners of modern newspaper editors generally adopted a more direct style than that of the courtier authors; but their accounts are shorter and in some ways less reliable.

Tullio Bulgarelli has analyzed the development of Italian printed journalism during the cinquecento in an introductory essay to his *Gli avvisi a stampa a Roma nel Cinquecento: bibliografia-antologia* (Roma: Istituto di Studi Romani, 1967). His term "avvisi" designates news bulletins, and the bibliography aims at including all of those published in Italian during the sixteenth century that are now preserved in Roman libraries, whatever the place of publication and whatever the nature of the news. Accounts in verse are somewhat arbitrarily excluded as belonging to literature rather than to journalism, as are also some particularly elaborate festival *livrets*. Accounts appearing some time after the event seem to be omitted also as not fitting into the category of bulletins.

The news is of many kinds; there are reports of battles, of diplomatic negotiations and treaties, of natural disasters, and of miraculous or portentious occurrences, as well as of celebrations. Most of these publications, generally rather brief, were meant to be hawked in the street or sold at the printer's shop. Bulgarelli points out that Pietro Aretino's comedy *La cortigiana*, from 1535, has a Roman character named Furfante, or "Rascal," one of whose activities is apparently the selling of newssheets. Authors of short *avvisi* who recount what they have seen must often have obtained their main reward from sales, rather than a patron, while those who composed longer, more elaborate *livrets* probably continued to receive compensation from official sources. As for the "editors" who put together news from elsewhere, like the prolific Bernardino Beccari at the Nicolò Mutii house in Rome, one presumes they were paid by employers, through wages or commissions. They may, however, have had considerable freedom in choosing subjects and determining the form and tone of their accounts.

Of the 254 *avvisi* in Bulgarelli's bibliography, 100 deal with *feste*, a fact that shows the prevailing interest in such matters. While all these are in Italian, only 72 report celebrations in Italy, the remainder having to do with festive occurrences abroad, especially in France and Spain. If the list is complete, or nearly so, for the holdings of Roman libraries, it is far from including all Italian festival *livrets* that have survived, much less all that appeared. I have examined in other cities at least 80 that do not figure in the bibliography, and have heard of, but not seen, some dozen more.[10] There must also be some extant ones of which I have not heard, but not, I venture to say, a great many. The total of surviving cinquecento *livrets* in Italian that deal with Italian celebrations may reasonably be put at near 200.

It is not easy to speculate about the number that have disappeared. Elaborate *livrets* might be kept as books of value, but the shorter *avvisi*, much more numerous, were not always the sort of publication that purchasers would think worthy of preservation. It is probably safe to suppose that as many as 50 have been lost, raising to some 250 the number that were printed. Some of the lost ones may have had to do with important events of pageantry in the first half of the century for which we have found no printed account, such as the meeting of Pope Leo X and King Francis I at Bologna in 1515, or the triumphal entry of the emperor Charles V into Palermo in 1535, or the visit of King Henry II to Turin in 1548. Others may have dealt with less important, undocumented events in the last five decades, or might bring further information concerning major occasions for which one or more *livrets* are already known.

If festival accounts participated in the early development of modern journalism, they also constitute, especially in the more elaborate examples, a kind of literary genre, with its own literary conventions and preferred structure. The author is endeavoring to share with a friend or a patron an experience that had filled him[11] with admiration and esthetic pleasure. Or he is recording for the outer world and posterity the extraordinary accomplishment of his native city in its magnificent reception of an august personage. His discourse includes some or all of the following components:

1. A summary of circumstances leading up to the triumphal event.
2. An account of preparations by the city government or local prince for the reception of the honored guest or *triumphator*, with a description of *apparati* constructed at the city gate and in the streets.
3. A description of the procession of local dignitaries who go out through the city gate to meet the guest.
4. A description of the procession that comes back in through the gate, with the local party preceding the visitors.
5. An account of the procession's progress through city streets to the duomo, and thence to the palace assigned for the guest's residence. The description of *apparati* is sometimes included here rather than in the account of preparations.
6. An account of subsequent ceremonies and entertainments during

the guest's stay in the city, including banquets, dramatic skits, and, sometimes, lavish productions of comedies or other "literary" dramas.

The information about preparations is nearly always far less full than modern students would like it to be, and sometimes it is omitted altogether. The description of the *apparati* is also often scanty, particularly in the early decades. The authors were not always greatly interested, and sometimes did not have the humanistic education required to understand the details of street *apparati*, with their architectural structure in imitation of the Ancients, their painted and sculpted allegories, and their erudite Latin inscriptions. It is not unusual in the first half of the century, to find that authors have passed over intricate decorations with such barren qualifications as "of very triumphant appearance," or "with many pleasant and learned stories." In later decades, with the growth of humanistic knowledge in such fields as emblematics, and the establishment of a recent, neoclassical tradition in triumphal entries, reporters gave more attention to such things. Occasionally, as at Milan in 1598, the *livret* was written by the humanist who had planned the *apparati*.[12] In such cases the commentary can be particularly detailed and valuable.

The component found most consistently in *livrets*, and the one most important in the minds of many authors, was the description of the procession, with detailed attention to costumes and the order of precedence. These matters, distant from the primary concerns of most modern students, were intensely interesting to contemporary spectators and readers. Much money was spent on special costumes, such as, for example, the identical ones made for the 30 or 50 young men of good family who were usually appointed to greet an honored guest outside the city walls and "serve" him during his visit. City officials and doctors of law wore colorful costumes that are but faintly echoed in the gowns and hoods of today's academic processions; and the clergy were naturally in their most stately array. Everyone who rode in the procession—if not everyone who walked—wore his best, often specially made for the occasion. The saying "clothes make the man" was, of course, far more valid in the Renaissance than today. The variety of dress was much greater, and one could tell a person's social station, if not his actual office, at a glance, even on an ordinary day. Such distinctions were still more evident at times of ceremony. In the papal procession at Ferrara even the beasts of burden wore distinctive blankets.

Like costumes, the order of the procession was also much remarked and commented upon. Disputes of precedence were common on ceremonial occasions, most notably between ambassadors of different states, such as Florence and Genoa, or Spain and France.

Noblemen or townsmen who cut distinguished figures in the procession were pleased to have their costumes described and their ceremonial positions recorded in the *livret*, and were, no doubt, among its purchasers. Perhaps copies were also bought and sent to relatives in other cities.

The reporting of later entertainments, in the evening after the entry and on subsequent days, is often succinct, but may extend to a description of banquets and the transcription of recited verses. Occasionally even the text of a comedy or other play written for the occasion is reproduced, and in such cases *livrets* become important sources of literary history.[13] Usually, however, such plays are published separately, if at all.

If the most elaborate festival *livrets* often show signs of conforming to the conventions of a literary genre, it follows that they cannot always be taken as objective reporting. This fact was pointed out by the festival scholar W. McAllister Johnson in a provocative paper given at a Tours colloquium in 1972.[14] The shorter accounts done by editors in a printing shop may be no more reliable; for if the courtier authors are eager to please their patrons and the protagonists of the pageantry, the journalistic ones are equally careful to say what is favorable to those in authority, while striving also, of course, to interest readers. Freedom of the press has scarcely been conceived of, much less established. Thus crowds in the streets will always be reported as having been ecstatic in their greeting of entering sovereigns, and the latter are always greatly moved by their welcome, by the majesty of the city they are visiting, and by the beauty and ingenuity of the street decorations.

It is, of course, appropriate to take such assertions with a grain of salt, but one may also carry skepticism too far. Neither the crowds in the streets nor learned observers saw civic pageantry with the jaded eye of the twentieth century. Unlike the entertainments of the modern theater, cinema, and television, triumphal entries were rare spectacles, seldom occurring in a given city more than once in a decade. Ferrara's five in 1598 are almost unique. The experience was not a common one even for princes. French kings, for example, customarily made *joyeuses entrées* into the principal cities of the realm soon after their accession, but welcomes on subsequent visits were far less elaborate. Italian princes might have a formal entry on their accession; and their brides were received triumphally only once, at the time of marriage. Extraordinary occasions for triumphal entries, such as fresh conquests, or summit conferences between popes and sovereigns, were also rare.

The unrivalled champion in triumphal experiences was the emperor Charles V, who travelled frequently over his wide dominions and elsewhere, between 1515 and 1541, and was received with maximum pomp in Flanders, Spain, Italy, Germany, England, and France. Even he, however, made no more than about two dozen grand entries into cities. He is reported as having been unfailingly interested in entry *apparati*, as also in local cathedrals and palaces, and seems to have been in fact a man of superior cultural and geographical curiosity. Like other conscientious princes, he was also aware of playing a role in a civic drama.

As for the crowds in the *piazze* and streets, their curiosity must have been intense, not just for a sight of the grand personages of the procession (whom they could not know in advance from photographs, and were unlikely to have seen in painted portraits), but also for the learned representations of the *apparati*. A number of *livrets* report that townspeople spent time inspecting the decorations in the days preceding entries, and sometimes the constructions were left intact to be admired for some days afterward. We should not dismiss as insincere such fervor as that of a man describing the theater built for the Roman Campidoglio celebrations of 1513, who says, in the supreme hyperbole of the time, that the Ancients have been equalled. Aged invalids who may never leave their beds again have been carried to see the construction and declare that they have never seen anything like it. Matrons who never go out except to church have also been taken to the site, along with young children, who were doubtless admonished to imprint what they have seen on their memories.[15] Even on the most august occasions, many people no doubt remained aware of social injustices and of political hypocrisy, but this awareness did not preclude esthetic enjoyment of artistic creations and civic drama, and it is probable that the enthusiasm of most authors of *livrets* is sincere.

A different kind of inaccuracy arises when authors represent ceremonies or street decorations as having been better ordered or more nearly perfect than had in fact been the case. There were often hitches in ceremonies, as a result of insufficient rehearsal or planning, or because of the disrupting pressure of crowds. Rain ruined costumes and broke up the order of processions. Quite often there was not enough time for completion of street *apparati*, as the Italian travel plans of princes such as the touring Charles V or the campaigning Louis XII were settled and made known too little in advance. Sometimes the chroniclers lament the fact that things were not finished. The humanistic and rather pedantic author of one particularly elaborate *livret* is frank in stating that he is going to describe *apparati* as they would have been if there had been time to do things properly.[16] Other authors doubtless did the same without saying so. For cultural historians, this kind of inaccuracy is, however, less serious than might first be thought, since what was planned can be quite as interesting and significant as what was achieved.

The vogue of the festival *livret* was far from over at the end of the cinquecento. The baroque fêtes of the seventeenth century were often recorded in elaborate volumes with elegant typography and handsome engravings made possible by technical progress in the printer's art. Still later, in the late eighteenth and early nineteenth centuries, political changes brought about by the French Revolution and the Napoleonic Empire gave rise to new forms of pageantry in Italy as well as in France, and one can learn much about the intellectual climate of that time from its festival *livrets*.[17] Books commemorating state pageantry continue to be prepared even today, but those done after about 1850 do not match the importance of earlier ones as documents of cultural history.

The Ferrarese Tradition
of Pageantry and Courtly Entertainments

Special political circumstances combined to make 1598 an extraordinary year for state pageantry in the Italian city of Ferrara. While it would be insufficient to say that this blaze of pomp and ceremony was either the last flicker of one brilliant period or the first of a new one, there is some truth in both views. Because the year saw the end of centuries of rule in Ferrara by the often brilliant Este family, Renaissance scholars in various disciplines have tended to see it as a terminal date, sometimes to the point of showing little interest in the city's cultural and political fortunes thereafter.

During the period of Este rule, from the thirteenth century, or at least from the early quattrocento, Ferrara had indeed played a cultural role in medieval and Renaissance Italy quite out of proportion to its size and economic importance. The lords of the city — first just *signori*, then marquesses, then dukes — had employed talented artists in the decoration of the Castello and other palaces of the city and its environs; and in the late fifteenth century, particularly in the time of Duke Ercole I, the court of Ferrara had also led Italy in the revival of classical comedy, with performances first of Plautus in translation, then of original compositions in Italian. Ercole's daughter Isabella d'Este had taken her passion for the theater to Mantua on becoming marchioness of that city, and through other family relations had encouraged the staging of comedies also in the little court of Urbino. During the sixteenth century Ferrara saw the production of tragedies and pastoral plays as well. In the late quattrocento and early cinquecento, a pair of poets patronized by the Este, Matteo Boiardo and Ludovico Ariosto, had also given two of the first and finest compositions in the new, peculiarly Italian genre of the *poema cavalleresco*, or mock chivalric epic. Ariosto, the author of comedies and satires as well as of the *Orlando furioso*, has more claim than any Florentine, except perhaps Machiavelli, to being designated as the primary literary figure of the Italian High Renaissance. Later, during the second half of the century, in the Counter-Reformation, Torquato Tasso wrote most of the Christian epic of the *Gerusalemme liberata* under Este patronage (although relations with his employers were often unhappy and he was actually in prison for part of his stay in the city).[18] The Este were also often the foremost patrons of music among Italian princes, keeping considerable numbers of composers, instrumentalists and singers at home and inviting other famous ones to visit the city.[19]

Like Urbino, whose court in the early cinquecento is the setting of Castiglione's *The Courtier*, and perhaps more than Florence, at least until the time of the Medici grand dukes, Ferrara was distinguished by the refinement of its courtly entertainments. It was remarkable not only for major theatrical productions, costly and usually well recorded, but also for such less memorable entertainments as small-scale concerts, short dramatic skits, and refined but simple diversions like listening to cantos of Ariosto's *Orlando furioso*.

Most courtly entertainments can be distinguished from pageantry, although the two often arise on the same occasions, such as dynastic marriages, princely visits, or annual civic holidays. The Ferrarese tradition of civic pageantry was not so rich as those of Venice or Rome, much grander states, but the citizens were far from unaccustomed to majestic public spectacles. There was, of course, processional pageantry on certain annual religious holidays. Among these, the feast of the city's patron Saint George (April 24) was a rough equivalent of the Florentine San Giovanni or the Venetian San Marco, and the pageantry for the occasion had civic as well as religious content.[20] Irregular, exceptional occasions for pageantry arose also, as in other princely states, on the occasion of happy events in the lives of the rulers, or state visits from other princes. Borso d'Este, who pursued the Renaissance ideal of *magnificenza* with particular fervor, was the protagonist of some of the grandest ceremonies and processions in the early revival of the classical triumph.[21] In 1452, while still merely marquess at home, he was solemnly invested as duke of Modena and Reggio by the emperor Frederick III. The latter was visiting Ferrara on the way back to Germany from Rome, where he had himself just been crowned emperor by Pope Nicholas V. The investiture of Borso was preceded by a grand procession through the streets from the Castello, and took place in public view on a decorated tribunal specially constructed in the piazza before the cathedral. The crowds, who seem to have been genuinely fond of their flamboyant lord, and who must also have seen increased distinction for their city in his elevation, shouted "Duca! duca!"[22] The next year Borso formally entered Modena and Reggio, in two of the most remarkable classicizing *triumphi* of the century. City officials had had ample time for preparations, guided to some extent by messages from the duke himself and his Ferrarese courtiers. The Modenese *apparati* included, among other things, two elaborate triumph wagons. Reggio had still more allegorical chariots and floats, as well as stationary displays and dramatic *tableaux vivants* placed along the entry route. There were some remarkable "machines," such as one with ascending and descending angels that recalled the complicated stage mechanisms of late medieval religious drama.[23]

In 1459, back in Ferrara, Borso gave a triumphal state reception to Pope Pius II, en route to the Council of Mantua. In 1471, very near the end of his reign, he himself traveled to Rome to be invested by Pope Paul II as first duke of Ferrara. His entry into the Eternal City in preparation for that ceremony was another classical triumph, although with less in the way of special *apparati* than had been seen in Modena. According to the account of an Este courtier, Francesco Ariosti,[24] Borso impressed the crowd by his "imperial appearance" (*cesareo aspecto*). He was greeted at the edge of the city not only by ecclesiastical officials but also by the senator of Rome, who, although now a purely ceremonial official and traditionally a foreigner, recalled for native Romans the distant glories of the S.P.Q.R. This official too was dressed like a triumphant ancient emperor, and he was attended by 100 consular patricians, native Roman gentry. The chronicler Ariosti thought that if the emperor Caius Caesar or Augustus came back to enter Rome once again, they could receive no grander reception than that given to the "divine" Borso.[25]

No succeeding duke, perhaps, cut quite so fine a ceremonial figure, but the following century and a quarter saw a number of grand entries into Ferrara itself, as such manifestations became more common throughout Italy and in the rest of western Europe.[26] During the period of the "Italian Wars," 1494–1558, the city's geographical position and fortunate alliances spared it an overbearing visit either from the invading French kings or, later, from the victorious emperor Charles V, but Ferrara did receive a pope in 1543, and in 1574 it welcomed French king Henry III in friendly circumstances. There were triumphal receptions as well for five ducal brides.

Costumes were brilliant and costly from the earliest of the Ferrarese entries. The façades of houses were commonly adorned too by the hanging of tapestries, and the streets were often further transformed by the suspension of bright canopies; but there was in Ferrara as elsewhere a definite progression in the elaboration of special *apparati* built at city gates and in the streets. Those for Lucrezia Borgia in 1502 were still fairly simple: arches made of greenery, and stages from which actors recited verses, in the manner of some late medieval French royal entries. The first *ingresso* for which there were temporary architectural arches, in supposed imitation of ancient Rome, was apparently that of Paul III in 1543. Thereafter such arches were de rigueur for formal entries of important personages.

Five of the *ingressi trionfali* took place during the long reign of Alfonso II, the last duke (1559–1597), who equalled Borso in ambition and love of magnificence, if not in political accomplishments.[27] He was the son of Princess Renée de France and during his youth went to his mother's country several times in order to fight in the service of King Henry II. It was from France that he came home in 1559 upon learning of his father's death. He entered the city from the suburban palace of the Belvedere and was invested by the *Giudice*, head of the city fathers called *Savi*, after a ceremonial "election." By his own wish the entry and the investiture rites were given a formality and public character unmatched since the time of Borso. One motive for the unusual pomp, if one looks beyond a natural inclination of Alfonso's character, was an increasingly keen rivalry with the Medici of Florence, to whom the new duke had recently allied himself in marriage, but whom he and other Este saw as parvenus among reigning Italian nobility.

After the death of his first wife, Lucrezia de' Medici, Alfonso married a Habsburg princess, Barbara, at the same moment as the Medici heir apparent, Prince Francesco, married her sister Johanna. A longstanding dispute between the two families and states over ceremonial precedence flared up at joint wedding ceremonies in Trent. Ferrara's welcome of Barbara shortly thereafter was magnificent, with a grand entry and following entertainments that may have equalled those Florence had prepared for Johanna, much better remembered.[28] In a foreshadowing of 1598, the duke of Mantua arrived on the Po for a state visit, and Venice sent special ceremonial ambassadors. There was a series of banquets with courtly entertainments, including a *bagordo*, or sham battle, on one evening and, on another, a grand *torneo* called the *Tempio d'amore*. Verses for the *torneo* had been composed by the ducal secretary and historiographer Giovan Battista Pigna and several other poets, including the young Torquato Tasso, who had just arrived to enter the duke's service.[29]

Although less wealthy than the Medici, Alfonso was determined not to be outdone in *magnificenza*. Moreover, the theatrical tradition at the Este court was perhaps the best established in the peninsula.[30] It was honorably maintained during his reign, when dramatic entertainments at the Ferrarese court and in town houses or country villas were perhaps as frequent as anywhere in Italy. There were major performances for nearly all entries and state visits, and also on such lesser occasions as the elevation of Luigi d'Este to the rank of cardinal in 1561, the wedding of the duke's sister Lucrezia to the son of the duke of Urbino in 1570, and the visit of Luigi Gonzaga, prince of Clèves, in 1575. Most years there were also elaborate dramatic productions for carnival. It was easy to become a connoisseur of theater in Ferrara.

Theatrical productions in the city during the High Renaissance were distinguished by a certain learned character, as the term *commedie eru-*

dite for imitations of Terence and Plautus suggests. There was, however, nothing pedantic about the tone of such plays, which perfectly suited the humanistic tastes of courtly audiences of the time. The physical splendor of Ferrarese productions, with gorgeous costumes and scenery, was also insurance against pedantry and dullness.

The city kept its prominent place at the forefront of innovation and experimentation in the theater in later decades, although Florence, Mantua, and some other cities now gave it strong competition. Performances were no longer confined mainly to *commedie erudite*, in which the Este court had pioneered. In the 1540s and 1550s, the learned Giraldi Cinzio, professor at the Studio and ducal secretary, directed student performances of several tragedies of his own composition. These performances took place in Cinzio's own house, but Duke Ercole II and perhaps the young Alfonso were present on at least one occasion. Until then the newly revived classical genre of the tragedy had been enjoyed only in the written text or through readings aloud in academic circles. Unfortunately, Giraldi's productions had relatively little lasting effect. Unlike neoclassical comedy, tragedy never really caught on in the Italian Renaissance. Humanists in various cities continued attempts to revive the genre, but it apparently did not at this time appeal to courtly audiences, as it would do a century later in France.

The case is very different for the pastoral play, in whose early history Ferrara also played an important role. Giraldi had written and produced one such play, the *Egle*, in 1543. In 1573 Torquato Tasso's *Aminta*, masterpiece of the genre, was produced at the Belvedere palace, just outside town on an island in the Po. (Tasso, who had first been in the service of Cardinal Luigi d'Este and was now in that of the duke, had not yet entered the period of mental torment that led Alfonso to confine him for years in the Castello and the Hospital of St. Anna.) The play was put on by the Gelosi, a company of travelling actors then becoming famous in northern Italy and France. They specialized in partly improvised *commedia dell'arte* performances, then still a relatively new dramatic form, but could also be hired to act out literary texts. Alfonso had had them to Ferrara for the wedding of his sister Lucrezia two years before, and was to invite them back on other occasions. He also employed them at great expense to entertain French king Henry III in Venice a year after the playing of the *Aminta*.

Ferrara was, as well, one of the centers for the development of the drama with music, soon to lead to the melodrama and early opera. Like his predecessors, Alfonso maintained a large and distinguished group of singers and instrumentalists,[31] and they were increasingly employed to support dramatic entertainments. Musical *intermedii* had been presented between the acts of comedies since the time of Ercole I; now music became better integrated with the dramatic action. Among the literary genres, pastoral plays seemed particularly appropriate for music. There had been music for Tasso's *Aminta*, as there would be also for Guarini's highly successful *Pastor fido*, which was written in Ferrara but received its first grand performance in Mantua in 1598.

The Ferrarese elite of Alfonso's time enjoyed as well another elaborate dramatic genre, eminently aulic or courtly in its nature and appeal. This was the *torneo*, also called, *abbattimento*, a mock chivalric combat on horseback which was done in time to music, had allegorical or literary content, and included the singing of verses.[32] There had been *tornei* in the quattrocento, but they had been simpler in form. Now court poets such as Tasso wrote verses and prologues for *tornei*, and the invention of the allegorical plots was of course also a literary matter. Costumes were extremely rich, and stage settings highly elaborate. The first performance for which there is a good description took place in 1561 in the courtyard between the Castello and the Palazzo Ducale, on the site of today's *Municipio*, as a part of celebrations honoring the new cardinal Luigi d'Este. This *torneo* was called the *Castello di Gorgoferusa*; often, in such dramas, a castle held by evil characters had to be assaulted. A second, called *Il monte di Feronia*, was staged three weeks later, partly for the visit of Prince Francesco de' Medici. These two early *tornei* and a third, the *Tempio d'amore*, one of the entertainments for the duke's 1565 marriage to Barbara d'Austria, were published in 1566 by the Ferrarese printer Francesco Rossi, with Agostino Argenti as editor, under a proud title beginning *Cavalerie della città di Ferrara* [Ariostea, BLL]. There were other *tornei* for later occasions, such as *L'isola beata*, done for a visit of Duchess Barbara's brother the Archduke Charles in 1569, and *Il mago rilucente*, performed for the marriage of the duke's sister Lucrezia to the duke of Urbino in 1570.[33]

Despite its fondness for *tornei*, Ferrara seems not to have been very familiar with a related courtly genre, that of the *ballet de cour*, beginning to flourish in France during this period.[34] That genre was apparently introduced, however, after the arrival of Alfonso's third duchess, the young Margherita Gonzaga, who was fond of all kinds of courtly entertainments.[35]

In addition to major performances of plays and *tornei*, Ferrarese court-iers enjoyed countless shorter dramatic skits, some given as *intermedii* between the acts of plays, and some done independently at balls or banquets. The variety of *divertimenti* at the Este court was remarkable, probably superior, for example, to that in Florence at the same time; and the refinement of taste in various aspects of the *vita cortigiana* must have been very great. It was fitting that a manual of courtly entertain-ment which enjoyed a considerable fortune in Italy and abroad dur-ing the second half of the cinquecento, Cristoforo di Messisbugo's *Banchetti*, should have been written by a citizen of Ferrara and first published there.[36]

Alfonso II also did his duty for the cause of learning in his capital, seeing to the proper support of the Ferrarese Studio, or university, and ordering an ambitious book buying program for the ducal library (now the core of the Biblioteca Estense, Modena). By maintaining a remark-able number of town palaces and country pleasure houses, and a per-sonal household of over three hundred persons, he kept up as well the standard of more ephemeral *magnificenza* in personal life style. If Fer-rara retained its place in the avant-garde of the arts and general cultur-al movements of the times, and the pleasures of its court were famous, the strain on the budget of what was but a middle-sized princely state came to be very heavy. The population may well have begun to resent its financial burden.

The Devolution

The achievements of Duke Alfonso in the cultural domain were not matched in the political one. Although he had family ties both to the Valois and to the Habsburgs, had fought with real distinction for France while young, and had later volunteered his military services to the em-peror as well, he was unsuccessful in efforts to use these high connec-tions for his own advantage or for that of his state. His ambitions had been great. When Henry of Valois abandoned the court of Poland in 1574 to return home to be king of France, Alfonso hoped to be chos-en as the Poles' new sovereign. As Henry prepared to cross northern Italy on his way home, the duke rushed to meet him in the Veneto and then took up so much of the young monarch's time during the royal visit to Venice that the government of the republic was understandably resentful.[37] Later he not only insisted that Henry make a detour to pass through Ferrara, for a magnificent and costly reception, but also stayed with the king on the subsequent journey as far as Turin. His Polish ambitions, however, came to naught.

By 1574, Alfonso was, in addition, much worried about his own succession, and his last years were dominated by that concern. He had had no children by his three wives, and his only brother, Luigi, was a cardinal and thus unmarried.[38] The duchy of Ferrara, unlike that of Modena and Reggio, was a papal fief, since Borso d'Este had obtained it from Paul II in the quattrocento. In 1567, perhaps already with Ferrara in view, Pope Pius V published a bull that forbade the transmission of papal fiefs to any but legitimate descendants. Where no such descendants existed, the fief would "devolve" to the pontiff and the States of the Church.[39] There had been little stigma attached to illegitimacy in the Italian Early and High Renaissance, but attitudes were changing. Alfonso made several fruitless efforts to get papal permission to name a successor in his will. In 1574, trying another tack, he almost managed to obtain an unrestricted imperial title to replace the papal one. Later, he nearly secured a change of Vatican policy from Gregory XIV. In the end, all diplomatic initiatives failed. Nevertheless, in a secret 1595 testament, Alfonso named his cousin Cesare d'Este as heir to the duchy of Ferrara, as well as to that of Modena and Reggio. The old duke died in the Castello at Ferrara on October 27, 1597.

Cesare d'Este was, like his dead lord, a grandson of Alfonso I. His father, the marquess of Montecchio, had been born of a union between that duke and a woman of common birth named Laura Danti. The union was illegitimate in the eyes of the papal authority (and most subsequent historians), but valid for Este apologists.[40] Cesare had not actually been a favorite of the dead Alfonso II, who had considered making another, much more distant Este cousin, named Filippo, the heir instead, and who delayed announcing his choice until virtually the last minute. During one of the last evenings of his life he finally summoned the chosen young man to his chamber to hear a reading of the will and to receive some hasty political advice.

Upon the duke's death, Cesare acted quickly. He transferred his residence from the handsome but relatively modest Palazzo dei Diamanti to the Castello, and set about having himself installed formally as the new lord of the city. The *Giudice* of the *Savi*, chief among the city fathers, had bells rung to summon magistrates and the heads of guilds to the

Palazzo Communale, adjacent to the Castello on the site of today's Palazzo del *Municipio*. There was to be a public reading of the will and a formal "election" of Cesare. Recent Este dukes had been careful to flatter the long-subordinate communal government by observing this form, and Cesare was particularly in need of popular support.[41] On the next day, October 29, he awaited the *Giudice* and other *Savi* in a public room of the Castello called the Sala della Stufa, seated on a throne in princely dress with a ducal beret and crown on his head. Upon entreaty, he agreed to become lord of the city and accepted from the *Giudice* two essential symbols of office: the sceptre and a naked sword.

Cesare then left the castle to proceed to the duomo, first showing himself at the top of the monumental stairway in the courtyard, and then mounting a silver-draped horse for a roundabout ride through crowded streets to the church. The Florentine ambassador rode on his right (perhaps because the new duchess was a Medici), and the *Giudice* on his left. At the main altar of the cathedral, the bishop of the city, Giovanni Fontana, awaited his lord with natural misgivings, but resigned to playing his role in the ceremony to follow. After hearing a mass, Cesare swore upon a Gospel presented by the *Giudice* to act as a just ruler of his people. He then received the episcopal blessing, and a Te Deum was sung. In the piazza outside, trumpets sounded to herald not just the happy announcement of the succession but also that of Cesare's having abolished some oppressive taxes instituted by hard-pressed Alfonso. (The poor state of the treasury made it unfeasible, however, to have coins thrown to the crowd from a balcony on the front of the duomo, as was popularly expected.) The duke remounted his horse to return to the nearby Castello, accepting new congratulations from the crowds along the way.

An ambassador was dispatched to announce the succession to the pope in Rome. Clement's mind in the matter was, however, made up, and he lost no time in taking energetic counteraction. He issued a proclamation that the duchy had devolved to the Church, sent a formal warning to Cesare, ordered the raising of an armed force to be commanded by his twenty-seven-year-old nephew Cardinal Pietro Aldobrandini, and finally, on December 23, employed his unique weapon of excommunication. This last action had a strong effect upon Cesare. The Ferrarese people, who heard the act of excommunication read aloud in their cathedral on the last day of the year by Bishop Fontana, were also much affected, and feared a general interdict that would deprive them of the sacraments. This fear united perhaps with dissatisfaction caused by Alfonso's years of heavy taxation to undermine Cesare's position at home.

Ferrara's situation also deteriorated on the diplomatic front, although the other states in northern Italy were not at all eager to have the territory of the Papal States enlarged.[42] Venice was particularly loath to see papal forces on its near southern border, and her ambassador to the Holy See worked diligently in Cesare's cause. In the event, however, no Italian state seemed willing to risk disturbing the political equilibrium of the peninsula by going to war against the pontiff. The emperor Rudolph II, who had recognized Alfonso's right to name a successor for Modena and Reggio in return for a considerable sum, was also basically sympathetic to the Este cause, but he lent no determined help in the matter. The aged Philip II of Spain was not keen to forward the temporal ambitions of the pontiff either, but he was ill-informed and did not, in any case, desire a confrontation. As for King Henry IV of France, he came out definitely in favor of devolution and even offered to send troops to support the papal forces. He was pleased to do a favor for the pope who had defied Spain to forgive his repented Protestant heresy three years before; and no doubt he hoped also to do some harm to Spanish interests by fishing in troubled waters. This cynical betrayal of cousins and old friends was a bitter shock to the Este and must also have had a considerable practical effect on wavering Italian states.

Ferrara was strongly defended and might have withstood a long siege from the papal forces now gathered at Faenza under the command of Clement's nephew Cardinal Aldobrandini had other circumstances been more encouraging. Cesare was, however, unsure of popular support in a long campaign, and seems to have remained personally very much upset by the excommunication. On the diplomatic front the irresolution or outright betrayal of his putative allies was in discouraging contrast to the absolute determination of his enemy. He decided to give in, and foolishly chose the elderly Lucrezia d'Este, sister of the late duke, and herself dowager duchess of Urbino, to negotiate with the cardinal.[43] This strong-willed lady, to whom he gave plenipotentiary authority, seems actually to have disliked him as she had disliked his father before him.[44] Perhaps she also considered that he belonged to an inferior branch of the family. She happened, moreover, to be already on excellent terms with the young cardinal. It is thus likely that she was not very zealous in defending the new duke's interests.

The main outcome of the negotiations was inevitable in any case: Cesare would have to give up all claim to Ferrara for himself and his family. In return, his excommunication was lifted (and a general interdict avoided), and the pope made no objection to his retaining the duchy of Modena and Reggio, which might have been lost after a major conflict. The departing prince was allowed to carry away most of the mobile Este family possessions, including the ducal library and the state archives. (As a result of this move, modern historians of medieval and Renaissance Ferrara spend much time at the Biblioteca Estense and the Archivio di Stato in Modena.)

On January 9, while negotiations were still under way, but some terms already settled, Cesare complied with the first requirement by calling the *Savi* and some other members of the Ferrarese patriciate to the Castello to tell them of his decision to give up the city. After a moving oration, he returned the ducal crown and sceptre to the *Giudice* for safekeeping. In this poignant way the officers of the *comune* received back for a new disposition the symbols of a signory that they and their predecessors had been entrusting to the Este lords since the time of Azzo I, almost four centuries earlier. In accord with a hard custom of the age, Cesare was also required to send his young son as hostage to the cardinal. On the fifteenth Duchess Lucrezia returned to the city with a detailed report on the agreements, and on that same day papal representatives arrived to witness the division of goods and make arrangements for the transfer of authority. With the conclusion of this month and a half of political drama following upon the death of Alfonso II, the old civic arrangements of Este Ferrara were gone forever, and the stage was set for the extraordinary year of civic and religious pageantry documented in this volume.

The Pageantry of 1598

January 28–29

The first *livret* chronicles the departure of Cesare d'Este and the triumphal arrival of Cardinal Aldobrandini, who had been made legate *a latere*, or special envoy of the pontiff, and was in effect the new governor of Ferrara, analogous to the governing legate in the nearby papal city of Bologna. It had been agreed that he would arrive on January

29, and that Cesare should have departed, with his entourage, before that time. Accompanied by his family, retainers, and closest courtiers, the former prince left for Modena during the late morning of the twenty-eighth, in good time for the cardinal with his troops and officials to make a grand entry in the afternoon of the next day. Cesare was said by the author of the *livret* to have shown no emotion, and by Faustini[45] not to have looked up from a letter he was reading on leaving the castle, but the Este courtiers who had decided to remain in the city were saddened and apprehensive as they watched the procession. Following the prince's departure, two notaries read aloud the fifteen articles of the treaty to the *Giudice* and *Savi* and other notables in the Palazzo del Comune, and these terms were then "published" from the main window of the palace overlooking the Piazza, after a heralding of trumpets.

The populace seized the occasion of the short interregnum to molest the city's Jewish population, which had usually been protected by the Este. A number of Este soldiers also took out their frustration by destroying some ducal property. And a large group of minor nobility tried to take advantage of the prevailing uncertainties to obtain access to the supreme offices of *Giudice* and *Savi*, traditionally reserved to an elite of the highest nobles.[46]

Heavy rains had washed out both bridges over the partly silted up branch of the Po that flowed by the city. It was decided to repair the one by the Castel Tedaldo for the cardinal and to commission welcoming *apparati* for the path of his arrival. The *Giudice* and *Savi* were responsible for all arrangements, although they sought advice from Bishop Mateucci, one of a group of papal officials who had already established themselves in town. At least some of the expense accounts have survived. At the bottom of all approved bills, the *Giudice*, Count Camillo Rondinelli, has written "facciasi," that is, "let it be paid." The principal artist employed was apparently Girolamo Faccini ("Fazino" in the records), a Ferrarese painter who has left works in the Castello, at the church of Santa Maria in Vado, and elsewhere in the city. He was in charge of a team working on the *apparati*.[47]

The information on these constructions and on the procession found in the printed *livret* corresponds rather closely to that in the manuscript journal of Filippo Rodi, who was accustomed to chronicling state affairs.[48] Because the *apparati* were not finished, Cardinal Aldobrandini spent the good part of a day whiling away time on the Este pleasure island called Belvedere, just outside the city walls near the bridge. He started into town in late afternoon, preceded by the guilds of the city, with bright new banners, and by most of the Ferrarese clergy. The *Giudice* and other *Savi* met him first across the river, then at the city gate, which, like the corresponding bridge, was called after the Castel Tedaldo. It had painted figures of Justice and Clemency, the latter quality being one which the city fathers particularly hoped to find in the character of their new governor. On being offered the keys to the city, we are told in the *livret*, the young prelate laughed "with a combination of majesty and affability." He rode a richly dressed mule under a *baldacchino* carried by eight of fifty young noblemen whom the city, following a widespread entry custom, had outfitted in special livery to meet and serve the honored guest. The cardinal was preceded by a cross, symbol of his office as legate, and was followed by the *Giudice* and *Savi*. This central segment of the procession thus symbolized in its pattern the new civic arrangements.

Inside the city, three principal arches or *portoni* had been constructed on the entry route. The first, at the Cantone San Giobe, was dedicated to Glory. At its top was a banner of the church, between representations of St. Peter and St. Paul. The arms of the pope were depicted as supported by figures of Glory and Honor, while those of the cardinal-legate were being held up by Concord and Peace. Sculpted figures of Justice and Diligence stood atop columns. Separate Latin inscriptions extolled the pontiff and his nephew for the virtues that had brought them victory. The second arch, at the entrance of the palace courtyard facing westward toward San Domenico (then a romanesque construction rather than the present baroque one), was devoted to Immortality. Along with more arms of the pope and cardinal, it had figures of History (shown in the act of writing), Sculpture, and Painting, which were seen as three vehicles, or paths, to immortality. The inscription magnified the "res gestae" of the two prelates, whose names would pass into eternity. The third arch or *portone* was inside the palace courtyard on the opposite, eastern side, on the spot of today's Volto del Cavallo, and adjacent to the monumental outside stairway. It was dedicated to Felicity and looked to the future. The papal arms were supported by Peace and Clemency, while Virtue and Honor held up those of the legate. The goddess Iris, personification of the rainbow, was shown chasing clouds from the sky. In the inscription, the S.P.Q.F., that is, the Ferrarese people and government, looked forward optimistically to permanent peace and serenity for their city.

The cardinal passed through this last arch into the Piazza del Duomo and then dismounted at the cathedral for devotions. One of the young noblemen who had carried the *baldacchino* seized this occasion to make off with it and with the mount the cardinal had ridden.[49] He was not pursued because a quaint centuries-old custom known all over western Europe allowed the rabble or other bystanders to "sack" the *baldacchino* and steal the mount of entering princes. The most powerful sovereigns, including the emperor Charles V, usually submitted to this custom. After his devotions in the church, the cardinal had thus to proceed the short distance to the Castello on foot. The banners of the Church were hoisted on the four towers of the great building.

February to Early May

As could be expected, the citizenry did not appreciate having to lodge and nourish the soldiers who accompanied the new governor, and everyone was glad to see most of them depart after a couple of days. The cardinal was slightly indisposed the day after his arrival, but rode around the city to see the sights on the day after that. On Tuesday, February 3, the *Giudice* and *Savi* dispatched six ambassadors to Rome to present the city's obeisance to Pope Clement, and related ceremonies continued at home. On Sunday, February 8, the cardinal attended mass in state at the cathedral and heard an oath of allegiance pronounced by the *Giudice* and *Savi*. During the service inside, coins were thrown to the crowd from the *poggiuolo*, or balcony, over the main front portal of the building, something Cesare had been too poor to have officials do during his own consecration two months before. Soon after his arrival, the legate also had the good political sense to reduce taxes, gaining in this way much public good will. And he pleased at least the people of his age by decreeing that the wearing of masks would be allowed exceptionally during that year's carnival, about to begin. He enjoyed observing the masked merrymakers in the company of some of the young Ferrarese who had attended him in the entry. Later, he presented these youths with money and with medals coined to commemorate the conquest of Ferrara, and created them all *cavalieri*, or knights.[50] A number of influential families were thus ingratiated. The general round of festivities and rejoicings was scarcely interrupted on February 13 by a state funeral given to the duchess Lucrezia, who had died hard upon the completion of her diplomatic mission and who, in indication of her views, had left the bulk of her fortune to the cardinal.

The special Ferrarese envoys dispatched to Rome were awaited outside the city gate by a large party of ecclesiastical officials and cavalry come to escort them into the city, and on the day after their arrival, they were received by an exultant Pope Clement in formal consistory with his cardinals. He accepted their allegiance graciously and granted some favors that they asked.[51] Against the advice of his counsellors, he had decided to go visit the newly acquired city himself. To defray the cost of the journey for the Holy Father and a huge entourage, the cardinals had to authorize removing from the treasury in the Castel Sant'Angelo the very large sum of one hundred and fifty thousand *scudi*.[52]

Detailed plans had to be made. Following a custom for solemn papal displacements, a consecrated Host, or *Corpus Domini*, was sent along one day in advance of the pope, in the charge of the pope's personal sacristan, Angelo Rocca, who, like all holders of his office, was an Augustinian monk. A special *livret* was published in advance to prescribe the ceremonies for the journey and receptions of the Host, as well as those for later receptions of the pontiff himself.[53] No doubt, this pamphlet was dispatched to ecclesiastic and civil officials of towns lying on the route of the journey, and people in other places read it too as an interesting news bulletin. The fact that it was published in four different cities is an indication of the general curiosity as to its information. Long papal journeys did not occur every year, or every decade, and public interest was intense. Special *avvisi* were also to be printed after the fact to recount the separate progresses of the sacrament and the pope.[54]

The preliminary pamphlet prescribed that the Host, consecrated by Pope Clement at the high altar of Saint Peter's, was to be carried through the streets of Rome and other towns in a crystal container resting on the back of a pony. It was to be met at the gate of each city by the local bishop and his clergy, who would escort it to the duomo. At the moment of departure, they would accompany it as far as the gate through which it was to continue its journey. The pope, usually arriving the next day, was to be greeted by civic officials at the city gate, and by the local bishop or ranking prelate at the high altar of the duomo. Before each urban entry, he would pause to change his travelling clothes for pontifical costume.

After consecrating the departing Host in Saint Peter's on Sunday, April 12, Clement said another mass in the basilica on Monday the thirteenth before setting out himself. All resident cardinals accompanied him through the city to the Porta Angelica, and a number continued on with him. The great party of travellers took a much frequented indirect path toward the north, heading for the Adriatic coast through the territory of the Papal States and that of the duchy of Urbino (which was itself to devolve to the Church in 1624). Progress on the ponderous journey was steady, with the pontiff seldom staying more than one night in a place. There were elaborate ceremonial receptions almost everywhere, with the grandest entry *apparati* recorded for Narni (April 15), Foligno (April 18), Camerino (April 19), Ancona (April 26), Senigallia (May 1), Fano, the pope's home city (May 2), and Pesaro (May 3). Cardinal Aldobrandini came to meet his uncle in Ancona. In Rimini, on May 4, Clement graciously received Cesare d'Este, who had come from Modena to pay his respects and to be assured of the papal pardon.

May 7–8

The *Corpus Domini*, travelling ahead under the charge of Sacristan Rocca, reached the church and monastery of San Giorgio, just outside the southern walls of Ferrara,[55] on May 7 and was reverently received there by the local clergy. Rocca paused to await Clement at San Giorgio, for the Host was to be carried just ahead of the pontiff in the grand entry procession. In a learned treatise about the ritual to be observed in formal journeys of the *Corpus Domini* that he published the next year,[56] Rocca included an account of his own accompaniment of the Host to Ferrara, a second one of the papal entry, and a third of his own return journey to Rome with the Host at the end of the year. A handsome engraving in the first pages of the little book (figure 1) shows a part of the procession that accompanied the Host on its journey, with the sacristan riding solemnly behind his precious charge, holding his *ferula*, symbol of office, in his right hand. Another engraving in Rocca's book (figure 2) shows the papal entry into Ferrara, with the Sacristan riding prominently just behind the Host and just ahead of the cardinals. This second engraving is similar to, although not identical with, a separately published engraving of the entry procession by Antonio Tempesta, a small, differing part of which is reproduced in figure 3.

The pope with his entourage of ecclesiastics and Roman civic officials arrived at San Giorgio the same evening, May 7. Many people came out of the city to see him, but Clement slept at the monastery that night in preparation for making a solemn entry the next day. He waited then until three hours before sunset—a popular time for staging entries—before setting out on horseback, preceded by the consecrated Host under a white *baldacchino*.[57] In the middle of a bridge leading over the Po to the city gate named for San Giorgio, he was met by the *Giudice* and *Savi* who presented the keys to the city. At the gate itself, which had received new wooden doors for the occasion, he changed into pontifical dress, including a heavy mitre said to be worth half a million *scudi*, easily several million of today's dollars. Then he mounted a *sedia gestatoria* for the entry proper, which was to lead him, like all Renaissance *triumphatores*, first to the city's duomo and then to his appointed residence, the Castello Estense. The *sedia* was carried on the shoulders of eight *palafrenieri*, and the *baldacchino* by eight Ferrarese *dottori*.[58] Clement was preceded through the town by the *Corpus Domini* under another *baldacchino* entrusted to clergy; by the *Giudice* of the *Savi*, with thirty young men in special costumes; and, more closely, by a treasurer tossing specially minted coins that commemorated the "recuperation" of Ferrara.

The first arch, at the "Rastrello della Montagna," was topped by a large chiaroscuro painting that Faustini declares to have been the work of Ippolito Scarsello.[59] That attribution is, however, not borne out by the rather full records of expenses that have survived.[60] These make it apparent that the principal artist involved, director of a team, was Domenico Mona, who has left work in the Ferrarese churches of San Paolo, San Francesco, and Santa Maria in Vado. Other artists mentioned in the records who are identifiable in the Thieme-Becker *Lexikon* are Giulio Belloni, Gian Andrea Ghirardoni, and Andrea Pellizone.[61] It seems clear that for this entry, as for the earlier one of the cardinal, the city government commissioned mostly local artists, rather than sending to other cities, such as Bologna or Florence, for more celebrated men.

In the Via della Ghiara was a second arch, made of greenery rather than of simulated stone, with trophies of war hanging from branches. A third arch had been placed at the Via Saraceno. Three more, presumably small, were erected together at a crossroads near the church of San Francesco. At the head of the great street of the Giovecca, next to the

Castello, could be seen a tall column like that of Trajan in Rome. Turning left, the procession passed into the piazza in front of the cathedral, where the pontiff was awaited by more clergy and more troops. He alighted at the door of the great church and was received by Bishop Fontana, whose loyalty to Rome was now being rewarded. Clement proceeded to the main altar amid the sounds of a Te Deum performed by his own musicians from Rome. At the conclusion of ceremonies and religious services, he changed out of pontifical dress, came out of the cathedral and mounted a white pony for the short ride to the Castello. There he accepted the keys from the *castellano*, expressing his emotions both with tears and with laughter.[62]

Celebrations continued for several days, although on May 9 there occurred an accident which seriously altered the climate of rejoicing and mutual trust. Some Romans who had been accustomed to setting off fireworks from the summit of the Castel Sant'Angelo on holidays, prepared and lit a *girandola*, or fireworks wheel, atop the Torre Marchesana, the tower on the southeast corner of the Castello. The roof of the tower caught fire, and when a group of Ferrarese who did service as firemen arrived to fight the blaze, they were locked in the tower, by mistake or by malice. All perished. The pontiff, who had fled the Castello for fear that the fire and resultant clamor meant the beginning of an insurrection, later paid indemnities to the widows of the firemen.[63]

Clement set himself seriously to the task of establishing new governmental structures for the city and territory. There was a new communal council, subject ultimately to the authority of the cardinal-legate, but having important responsibilities nevertheless. Later, like the neighboring papal city of Bologna, Ferrara would obtain the right to send an ambassador to Rome. Clement stayed more than six months in the city, transacting not only local business but also that of the Holy See, giving illustration to the saying "Ubi pontifex, ibi Roma."

Not long after his arrival he learned of a new general peace between France and Spain that had been signed at Vervins in Picardy on May 8. This agreement had been promoted by papal agents, and the report of its conclusion delighted Clement, who was decidedly having a good year. He ordered processions of thanksgiving in the streets of Ferrara, just as he would have done in Rome, and went personally to give thanks in the church of San Francesco.[64] The rejoicing in the streets was sincere, for news of the treaty had cheered people all over Catholic Europe (if not the English and Dutch, who were losing a powerful ally against the Spaniards). People in Italy, as in Flanders, hoped for a long period of peace, and this hope contributed to the festive spirit of many civic celebrations in Ferrara and elsewhere during the following fall and summer. Several regular ambassadors to the Holy See had accompanied Clement to Ferrara, and special ambassadors began to arrive there soon after his settling in, some to conduct special business, but most sent only to congratulate him upon his victory and new acquisition. The pontiff received them all magnanimously in the Castello, ex-Estense. An imperial envoy arrived the very day of the papal entry. On May 15 there were ambassadors from Lucca, and on May 30, the four special ambassadors from Venice whose entry is recorded in our second *livret*.[65]

May 30

It was the custom of the Venetian signory to send a special embassy to foreign princes on their succession or on other occasions calling for congratulation.[66] The Republic of Saint Mark was, in fact, chagrined at the disappearance of the buffer state of Este Ferrara, and the northern advance of papal territory, but with the fait accompli its prudent government acted as always in accord with the artificial ritual of Renaissance diplomacy; it congratulated its victorious adversary. The pope was, of course, quite aware of the Venetians' true feelings about his acquisition of Ferrara—and their still stronger ones about his occupation of the disputed town of Comacchio—but by congratulating him they put him under reciprocal obligation. As social historian Richard Trexler has remarked in regard to a partly analogous Florentine congratulation of French king Charles VIII on the conquest of Naples, "Insincerity was in a sense converted to sincerity through ritual."[67]

The ambassadors from the great maritime republic were no doubt magnificently attired. They came from the north and entered the city through the Porta degli Angeli. The author of the *livret*, Gieronimo Amarotti, makes a point of recording that they had been greeted ceremonially outside the gate by Cardinal Aldobrandini, by Venetian prelates who were members of the Roman curia, and by a number of Ferrarese noblemen. All these people rode back into the city with the ambassadorial party, which, Amarotti tells us, included two hundred carriages. No triumphal *apparati* seem to have been constructed for reception of the ambassadors, but there were doubtless hanging tapestries and other decorations on private houses. The pontiff could not properly disturb himself to meet the four envoys in the street, but he is said to have watched the procession from behind louvered windows. The next day he received the noble Venetians and, a bit later, entertained them at supper, having them placed at a table near his own.

The ambassadors stayed, however, in a monastery, that of Saint Andrew. Lodging was extremely scarce in the city, with the huge papal entourage, and the large households of various special and ordinary ambassadors. It was to become still scarcer a few days later, on June 4, with the arrival of advance agents of the duke of Mantua, Vincenzo Gonzaga.

June 5

The Gonzaga had been friendly neighbors and relatives of the Este for many years, and the two courts were closely associated in various cultural developments of the Renaissance, most notably in movements of the theater and of music. Alfonso II's widow, the dowager duchess Margherita, was a Gonzaga and had returned home to Mantua after her husband's death (although she was to pay a visit to Ferrara during the pope's stay). Duke Vincenzo himself had been a companion of Cesare d'Este in youthful carouses and adventures. Like the Venetian government, however, he had stopped short of giving Cesare military support, and he adapted well to the fait accompli of papal conquest. Moreover, he and his aunt the dowager duchess were having some disputes with Cesare over family property, and hoped for Clement's benevolence in the matter.[68]

The duke came to Ferrara by water, travelling in a state vessel called a bucentaur, like the great ceremonial galley of the doge in Venice.[69] Both Mantua and Ferrara were near the main channel of the Po and could be reached from the large river via smaller waterways. Mantua, ten miles distant from the Po, is bounded on three sides by lakes made from the tributary Mincio. Ferrara is several miles south of the river, to which today it is connected in part by an artificial waterway. In the sixteenth century the city was situated on a fairly important branch of the river, which begins splitting in Emilia to form a wide delta. One could embark at the very edge of the city, or at a more important port on the main channel at Pontelagoscuro. Dukes of Ferrara, who had also possessed bucentaurs, could float down the river to the Adriatic, then up the coast to Chioggia, where another vessel could be taken across the lagoon to Venice.[70] Vincenzo himself was to lodge in the Castello as guest of the pope, but his agents had come to Ferrara a day early in order to prepare a palace for other members of his large party.

On June 5, the duke disembarked at the Ponte Aucura—perhaps near Pontelagoscuro—and was greeted there by ten cardinals and a party of Ferrarese nobles. After ceremonial salutations, the cardinals returned to town, then at three hours before sunset the duke's procession set out under a drizzling rain toward the northern city gate called the Porta degli Angeli. Once within the walls, it passed through streets adorned by hanging tapestries and, we are told, by beautiful women leaning from windows. It was led by six trumpeters in the duke's livery, followed by mounted pages also in livery. Noblemen from Mantua and Casale Monferrato[71] were resplendent in specially made costumes, astride horses whose trappings were embroidered with gold and silver. The duke rode in a carriage upholstered in black velvet that had been lent by Cardinal Aldobrandini. The whole procession included four hundred horsemen and two hundred carriages, as well as numerous soldiers on foot. Vincenzo alighted at the Castello and was received by the pope and assembled cardinals in a great room that performed the function of the Sala del Consistorio in the Vatican Palace. After the young duke had knelt to kiss the feet of the pontiff, according to established ritual, he was himself raised up and kissed on both cheeks. Before retiring to the apartments prepared for him and twenty gentlemen retainers, the duke then paid his respects to the cardinals, who liked to be treated as the equals of all temporal sovereigns except the emperor. The rest of the Mantuan party had gone on to the rented palace, where the duke's cousin Ferrante Gonzaga was to serve as host of entertainments and banquets to which even the poor of Ferrara were admitted.

June 29

The Feast of Saints Peter and Paul, June 29, saw two unrelated celebrations and displays of pageantry. The first was sponsored by the duke of Sessa, Spanish ambassador to the Holy See, who was living in the

Palazzo dei Diamanti, formerly the private home of Cesare d'Este. It was a feudal custom on this feast day for the kingdom of Naples to present the pope with a *chinea*, or hackney horse. The ceremony, called the *acchinea*, normally took place, of course, in Rome, but the duke was pleased to observe it this year in Ferrara. He gave a huge banquet, with such striking dishes as whole peacocks, deer, and foxes, and a large pastry model of the Castello. His troops and retainers also staged a parade and military display, called an *armeggiare*.[72]

At the end of the day, there came another duke, Ranuccio I Farnese of Parma and Piacenza. The Farnese were parvenus in the eyes of other Italian ruling families, at a time when new importance was being given to antiquity of blood-line and position. The family stemmed from Pope Paul III, who in 1545 had alienated the territory of the duchy from Church possessions in order to give it to his descendants. In the early years Farnese rule had been disputed by the emperor Charles V, who held most of Lombardy, and by local nobility. Ranuccio's father, Alessandro, had greatly added to the family's standing by service as a general for Spain's Philip II in the Low Countries, but the dukedom still did not seem entirely secure, and the example of Cesare d'Este's deposition must not have been reassuring. Nor did Ranuccio have uniformly warm relations with all his noble neighbors. In 1598, he and Vincenzo Gonzaga were, in fact, bitter enemies, as a result of the latter's having repudiated his first wife, Margherita Farnese, Ranuccio's sister. These circumstances, the relative newness of the Farnese dukedom, and the rivalry with the duke of Mantua, perhaps explain the duke of Parma's efforts to make a uniquely magnificent impression.[73]

Similar motivations may explain the fact that three different *livrets* were published to describe the duke's journey and entry into Ferrara, more than were normally done even for the entries of popes or royal personages. Such magnificence had to be properly recorded, and the *livrets* were doubtless sent to various European courts. The one reproduced in this volume, written by the courtier Vincenzo Greco and published in Ferrara by Vittorio Baldini, who had become papal printer for the city, declares that Ranuccio had resolved to endow his journey and state visit with "that grandeur and splendor that were appropriate to his state and to his personage." A second account by Antonio Ianni da Ischia, printed in both Ferrara and Parma,[74] similarly emphasizes the expenditures incurred by the duke in the journey. The third account, dedicated to the duke's brother, Cardinal Lodovico Farnese, and done by Giovanni Paolo Mocante, or Muccante, a papal master of ceremonies, states that "perhaps even the Prince of Spain could not have made an entry so beautiful and so rich."[75] This was a supreme comparison in Counter-Reformation Europe. A more learned allusion was made by Ianni, who declared in a closing sonnet of his own composition that the state visit had been like an ancient Roman triumph on the Capitolium.

Ranuccio too came by bucentaur on the Po, from a greater distance than Vincenzo, and all three accounts emphasize the comfort and pleasures of the two-day journey (although Mocante, settled in Ferrara, could only know about them from hearsay). The duke had announced plans for the grand trip to his vassals (*feudatarii*) and had invited them to make arrangements to accompany him in proper state. Tailors in Parma and Piacenza must have had their hands full of orders. Ranuccio also caused great stores of provisions to be gathered for the journey and for later entertainments in Ferrara. Ianni lists some amounts: 800 sacks of flour, 160 barrels of wine, 200 of olive oil, 2,300 ordinary young chickens, 150 capons, 80 pairs of ducks, as well as some kids and boars, with 40 sacks of coal for cooking. A large number of ordinary river boats—forty-six according to Ianni, seventy or eighty according to Mocante—were gathered to carry provisions. At least one of them held ice from the mountains for the cooling of drinks on the journey. The ducal bucentaur, gorgeously decorated, carried a hundred musketeers as well as the duke himself and some of his nobles. It was preceded by two gunboats and followed by another.

On Saturday, June 27, the duke came out from Parma by carriage to an embarkation point at the mouth of the little Po tributary called the Parma. Taking leave of his brother, Cardinal Lodovico, who remained behind as regent, he mounted the ceremonial vessel, and the fleet set out. As it passed Brescello, some troops in the duke's service staged a military display on the shore. There could be no travel by darkness, and the fleet moored that night at Guastalla, the fief of the Ferrante Gonzaga who had accompanied his cousin Duke Vincenzo. There was a merry supper on board the bucentaur. Lunch next day was taken at Portiolo, in the territory of the duke of Mantua, who had sent an ambassador to welcome Ranuccio in his name. (He himself was by this time off on a visit to Venice.) Supper was at Massa, where the duke landed to get some exercise. On the next day, Monday the 29th, the Feast of Saints Peter and Paul, lunch was served under the trees in a pleasant wood belonging to a Benedictine abbey at Mezzano. Soldiers put on another display, and the company was amused by a buffoon, presumably a member of the duke's household. The atmosphere at this picnic was most relaxed, according to Ianni, "with no order of precedence." The party reembarked for the short remaining journey to the Ferrarese port of Pontelagoscuro. From there they went by land to an Este country house called the Isola, where the duke met a company of Ferrarese nobles who had come out to greet him.[76] Later, fourteen cardinals arrived, along with the ambassadors of the Empire, France, Spain, Venice, and Savoy. The cardinals returned to the city while the Ferrarese stayed on to take part in the entry. Two hours were required to organize the brilliantly attired procession, consisting not only of the duke's very large party but also of the Ferrarese welcoming delegation and numerous papal and Roman officials. It did not set out until an hour before sunset. The duke's costume was of tawny satin, with gold and silver embroidery, and there were diamonds on his velvet cap. After entering the city—presumably by the Porta degli Angeli, although we are not told—Ranuccio proceeded to the Castello, where he and his chief courtiers were admitted to kiss the pope's feet and to pay their respects to the cardinals, assembled in consistory. Then the duke was taken to his apartments, the same that had been given to Vincenzo Gonzaga. That same evening he paid formal calls on Cardinals Aldobrandini and San Giorgio, who ritually returned his visits before bedtime.

The procession had included 70 of Ranuccio's vassals and 40 of his knights, 250 adorned ceremonial horses, 100 musketeers, and 100 mounted lancers. The trumpeters numbered eight, in comparison to Vincenzo's six, and were dressed in scarlet livery. Cardinal Bentivoglio, who saw both entries, judged that Ranuccio had made the greater impression, in part because he was attended only by his own noblemen, while Vincenzo had some foreigners in his entourage.[77] The chronicler Guarini also awarded superior honors to Ranuccio.

During his stay in Ferrara, the duke entertained on a royal scale, both in his borrowed palace, and in the bucentaur, which was available for excursions and banquets. He had brought some musicians from his court, including the celebrated Claudio Merulo, to play for honored guests. At one lunch for Cardinal Aldobrandini, a thousand silver plates were used. Nor were the common people neglected. Greco states that special tables were kept provided with food for the poor, and on one day the duke gave a banquet for 130 German papal guards, who were induced, after ample ration of muscatel wine, to shout "Viva il Duca di Parma!" On departing the city, Ranuccio left handsome tips, including the large sum of 400 *scudi* for papal soldiers, and more for minor officials and servants. His return to Parma was effected over land, and he stopped off in Modena to discuss political matters with the deposed Cesare d'Este, who was doubtless eager for news.

Ranuccio's magnificence was not all occasional show. He was already a discerning patron of the arts at home, particularly of music and the theater.[78] There had been a number of lavish dramatic productions at the Farnese court, and in 1618, the duke was to commission the architect G. B. Aleotti to build a grand permanent theater in his Palazzo della Pilotta. This construction surpassed Palladio's Teatro Olimpico in Vicenza, from which it took its inspiration, and became perhaps the finest setting for dramatic performances in Italy. It survives today, newly restored, as the Teatro Farnese.

On the other side of the coin, the duke was far from commanding the loyalty of all his subjects or the respect of all his neighbors. In 1611 he had to suppress a conspiracy of local nobles who were receiving outside encouragement from his old acquaintances Vincenzo Gonzaga and Cesare d'Este. The grand visit to Ferrara had, however, been a diplomatic success in at least one quarter, for two years afterward, Ranuccio married the pope's niece Margherita Aldobrandini. The Farnese dynasty maintained itself in Parma until the second quarter of the eighteenth century, a little longer than the Gonzaga in Mantua, while in Modena the Este retained control, except for two short intervals, until the upheavals of the French Revolution.

August, September, October and Early November

In late August, 1598, two months after Ranuccio's visit, Pope Clement received the Spanish governor of Milan, Juan Fernández de Velasco, Constable of Castile. The constable was a personage more powerful than most Italian reigning princes, but he entered the city with modesty, pretending, says Cardinal Bentivoglio,[79] that he had taken ordinary transport on the post roads. He came, however, with a large company, and was received by the pope with appropriate courtesy and deference, staying in the Castello.

In late September Clement went to visit Comacchio, in a lagoon near the Adriatic. This port had been disputed between the Este and Venice, and the pope no doubt wished to emphasize his own new sovereignty there. While at this place, he learned of the death of King Philip II, which had occurred in Spain on September 13. During a very long reign, since 1556, that earnest monarch had dominated much of Europe, and the news of his passing made a strong impression. After his return from Comacchio, Clement attended a funeral mass for the Spanish king in the cathedral of Ferrara on October 13.

Near the end of his life, wishing to put the affairs of his family and his realms in order, Philip had arranged two dynastic marriages between Habsburgs of the Spanish and Austrian branches. His young son, the future Philip III, had been betrothed to Margaret, daughter of the archduke of Styria, and granddaughter of the emperor Ferdinand I. The old king's daughter Isabel was affianced to the archduke Albert, who had distinguished himself as a soldier in Flanders. Albert was giving up a cardinal's hat (which had not prevented his military service) in order to marry. This second marriage was almost as important politically as the first, for the bride and groom were to be the rulers of the southern Netherlands, which would be erected into a supposedly autonomous state. (The couple, known as the "Archdukes," did indeed reign there for many years, until the territory reverted to the Spanish crown on Isabel's death in 1633.)

Albert came from Flanders through Germany and Austria to join his cousin Margaret for a long, ceremonial journey across northern Italy and the Mediterranean to Spain.[80] Shortly before meeting, each learned of the death of Philip II. Margaret was now to be queen of Spain on her arrival, rather than just a princess, and was immediately hailed as such. Plans for the journey became more grandiose. It was to be the finest triumphal progress in Italy since French king Henry III had crossed from the Veneto to the Piedmont on the way home from Poland in 1574, and the finest triumph of Habsburgs in any country since Philip II himself had traversed Italy, Austria, Germany, and Flanders just a half century before, in 1548–1549. In splendor, if not in dramatic circumstance, it rivalled the emperor Charles V's majestic progress up the peninsula in 1535–1536, after his victories over Barbarossa in Tunis.

Cities likely to be on the route began to extend invitations and to start preparations. Most were either directly under Spanish rule, like those in the duchy of Milan, or within states that were clients of Spain,

such as the duchy of Mantua and the republic of Genoa. Venice and
its *terra ferma* conserved a much greater degree of independence, but
the signory meant, as always, to make a grand impression on the emi-
nent travellers. So also did the pope, who was anxious to strengthen
the young Habsburgs' already staunch devotion to the Roman church.
He offered to bless their coming matrimonial unions in a sort of preliminary marriage ceremony, called a *sposalizio*, at which the absent Philip
III and Isabel would be represented by proxies.[81] Such ceremonies were
commonly held for noble brides about to leave their home cities for
those of their husbands; but it was of course a rare honor to have one
performed by the Holy Father.

As cities made preparations to receive the exalted pair with appropriate ceremony and street *apparati*, a number of official and unofficial
chroniclers planned to record the royal visit. No fewer than fifteen *livrets*
would be published to commemorate the journey across Italy, and still
others for the arrival in Spain and entry into Valencia.[82]

Coming from different directions, the archduke and the future queen
met on October 29 in Trent, a city that was geographically a part of
Italy but politically included in the Empire. Both stayed in the Castello of the bishop-prince, Cardinal Lodovico Madruzzo. They were thence-
forth to travel together in so far as practical requirements allowed. The
queen's party is said to have included 800 human "mouths" (as well
as 200 horses and mules), while the archduke's included no fewer than
1600.[83] Many among the travellers required deferential treatment.
Margaret was accompanied by her mother and a number of Austrian
ladies, while Albert had enlisted Flemish ladies to help him go and
fetch the infanta. In small towns it was impossible for both parties to
be accommodated at once, and so one would precede the other by a
day, or they would lodge in different towns.

On November 3, the two parties arrived at Dolcè in Venetian territory. They were not going to Venice itself, but, in accordance with established custom, the republic appointed special ambassadors to see
the couple and their retainers through Venetian territory.[84] These
officials had practical as well as ceremonial duties; they would dash into
a town to see that the distribution of human provisions and hay had
been carried out properly, then go back a good way into the country
for their own lodging. When the queen and archduke arrived at the
Adige river, there was a triumphal arch with a welcoming inscription
over a specially erected bridge. The two Habsburgs then enjoyed Vene-

tian hospitality in or near Bussolengo from November 4 to 8. The queen received Cardinal Aldobrandini and the Spanish governor of Milan,[85] both of whom had rushed up to meet her. Before leaving Venetian territory, Margaret told the ambassadors that she would never forget their government's hospitality. The Republic of Saint Mark could in fact demonstrate matchless generosity and *magnificenza* when it wished to do so, and the queen was an impressionable young girl who may not have been the object of much attention before her betrothal. This was, however, only the beginning of her Italian progress.

On the ninth the couple crossed the Po to stay for three days at Revere, in the territory of the duke of Mantua. This prince had done a great deal of advance planning, eager, in the words of the author of the Mantuan *livret*, "to make the world know in all occasions ... the extraordinary devotion and reverence that [he] feels toward His Majesty [of Spain] and toward all the Most Serene House of Austria."[86] He had had a special new bucentaur constructed to lend to the queen, along with his usual one, for her travel on the Po and its tributaries. These boats had brought the Habsburg guests across the river from Venetian territory, would carry them on to Ferrara, and would later bring them back from from there on the Po and Mincio to Mantua. During their stay in Revere, Margaret and the archduke also received Cesare d'Este, now only duke of Modena and Reggio, who was perhaps anxious not to be forgotten by the Habsburgs.

November 12–18

On the twelfth the couple proceeded in the two bucentaurs, accompanied by many lesser vessels, to Pontelagoscuro near Ferrara.[87] They spent the night at the Este country house of the Isola, sending word that they would enter the city at two hours before sunset the next day. On the next morning, the thirteenth, two cardinals and some other dignitaries came out to wait upon the queen. At the appointed time, she got into a coach for a three-mile ride to the northern Porta degli Angeli. There she waited briefly in a specially constructed wooden tabernacle, fitted with a throne under a *baldacchino*, until all the cardinals resident in Ferrara came to fetch her. She rode a white horse in the entry procession. The engraving of Jacques Callot reproduced in figure 4 was done years later, for a *livret* recording Florentine funeral ceremonies for the queen in 1612, but it may be an accurate representation of an early moment of the entry. Most of the cardinals have already passed back through the gate into the city. Margaret has also apparently just ridden under the arch, for, most surprisingly, she herself is not shown. We see instead the archduke Albert riding between two cardinals, his horse being led by a groom. The queen's mother is following on a mare.

Special welcoming *apparati* had of course been constructed in the streets along the path of the royal entry. No records of payments to artists by the *comune* seem to have survived, but some partial ones of papal payments are preserved in the Archivio di Stato, Rome.[88] The Modenese painter Giovanni Guerra, who had probably come with the papal party from Rome, appears to have had the major responsibility. Giuseppe Cesari, known as the Cavalier d'Arpino, was also paid for work on this occasion. This artist, who had already been employed by Clement in Rome, was to do much more work there and hold a prominent position as head of the artistic Accademia di San Luca.

An inscription at the gate evoked the joy of angels and mortals at the royal visit. Inside the gate was a triumphal arch with other inscriptions hailing the approaching marriage. As the procession moved along the Strada degli Angeli, today's Corso Ercole I, toward the center of town, it passed painted figures of Religion, Justice, and Victory on the Palazzo dei Diamanti, temporary residence of the duke of Sessa, Spanish ambassador. A further arch *apparato*, extolling the virtues of the *Iugum Maritale*, adorned the entrance to the courtyard of the Castello. Margaret went upstairs into the presence of the pope in consistory with his cardinals (who had arrived just before her). She and her mother kissed the pontiff's feet before he raised them up in his own ritual gesture.

On the next day, the fourteenth, Margaret and Albert received formal visits from the cardinals. In the morning of the fifteenth, in a specially decorated papal chapel of the duomo, Clement said mass and performed the two ceremonies of *sposalizio*, Philip III being represented by the archduke, and Isabel by the duke of Sessa. The moment of Margaret's marriage is shown in the reproduced engraving by Raffaello Sciaminossi (figure 5) from the same 1612 funeral *livret*. The young man facing her, with his hand clasping hers, is the archduke, standing in for the king. The dowager archduchess can be seen in the background just behind Pope Clement. The remarkably graceful postures of these personages, along with details from the secular costumes of the courtiers, remind us that Italy was moving into the period of the baroque style.

In a separate ceremony after the *sposalizii*, Clement presented the queen with the Golden Rose, a symbolic award of merit that popes could confer upon individual personages who had rendered special service to the Church, or upon individual basilicas and cathedrals. It was not just a flower, but a whole rose bush, one or two feet high, with blossoms, leaves, and stems all in delicately worked gold. Such a *rosa d'oro* can be seen today in the treasure of the cathedral of Siena, among other places. In the sixteenth century these elaborate creations of the goldsmith's art seem to have been given often to noble ladies. In the preceding year, Clement had sent one to the Venetian *dogaressa* on the occasion of her coronation;[89] and the next year he was to confer another on Maria de' Medici, whose proxy marriage in Florence to King Henry IV of France was in fact performed by Cardinal Aldobrandini.[90]

In the evening after the marriage ceremonies, there was dancing, with maskings. But although the pope had lifted for one day the obligation of mourning for Philip II, the pious queen would not dance because she had taken communion that morning. On the next day the pope had a banquet for the two Habsburgs, and in the evening some women from Comacchio staged a regatta on the moat of the Castello. In the evening of the seventeenth, in the guards' room, there was the special performance of a play. It was not a comedy in Italian, or a *torneo*, or a pastoral drama, like those staged on so many special occasions by the Este, but a morality play in Latin, acted by pupils of Ferrara's Jesuit college, founded in 1551. One might indeed note that the old secular rulers were gone and that a Counter-Reformation pope had come to reside in their palace.

The Jesuit drama in Latin was composed and performed for the linguistic, rhetorical, and moral instruction of students. It was to reach its full development in the following century, but by 1598 had already been cultivated for several decades in Italy, Spain, France, and Germany.[91] There was some controversy within the order about the sort of plays to be presented, as well as about the proper way of performing them, and the first three editions of the *Ratio Studiorum* in 1586, 1591, and 1599 addressed the question. The more or less final provision in the matter is summarized in the following paragraph from 1599:

> The subject of tragedies and comedies, which must not be given except in Latin and on very rare occasions, ought to be sacred

and pious; and nothing should be introduced between the acts which is not in Latin and is not becoming; nor is a feminine role nor feminine attire to be introduced.[92]

The question of *intermedii* was a basic one. Short skits and dances between the acts of comedies and pastoral plays, usually with music, had acquired great prominence at the courts of the Este, the Medici, and other Italian princely families. Large amounts of money were spent on costumes and scenery, and lavishness was the rule. The tone was always light, and rarely edifying. Small wonder, then, that the leaders of the order should find it necessary to regulate such performances in their colleges.

The subject of the drama staged for the queen and archduke was the apocryphal Old Testament story of Judith and Holofernes. Like that of David and Goliath, this tale of a Jewish heroine who saved her native town by deceiving and then decapitating the infidel Assyrian general who was besieging it, was often appreciated by republicans as an illustration of a free people's defiance of tyranny. Such is, for example, the symbolism of Donatello's statue of Judith holding her enemy's severed head, which formerly stood in front of the Florentine Palazzo Vecchio. There could, however, have been no such implication at Ferrara in 1598. For the fathers and their students (as also for Martin Luther),[93] Judith was primarily an example of chastity and religious faith.

The name of the play's author is not recorded. Perhaps one of the local teachers had written it, but the text may also have come from elsewhere. In 1569 Father Stefano Tuccio had written and produced a *Giuditta* at the Jesuit college in Messina. This play had acquired a certain reputation, being performed also in Palermo and in Rome. Its author held a prominent position in the order during the last years before his death in 1597, being, among other things, one of the principal authors of the 1586 and 1591 editions of the *Ratio Studiorum*.[94] It is not unlikely that his was the play performed at the castle before the pious young queen; and in any case, an examination of the text of his play[95] will give us some idea of what the Ferrara performance must have been like.

Tuccio's drama was called a tragedy, but is certainly far from meeting the criteria of Aristotle or the Italian Renaissance critics inspired by him. The heroine is utterly without flaw of character, and is triumphant, rather than dead or disgraced, at the action's end. For us, the composition is more like a medieval morality play, and its subject had in fact already been treated in vernacular *sacre rappresentazioni*. Tucci's work is, however, classical in form, with a prologue, five acts, and an epilogue. No texts for *intermedii* have survived, but these were quite possibly planned specially for different performances. The play is a very discursive one, with long speeches in hexameters. The acts are interspersed, however, with choruses using briefer verse forms, and the principal characters also occasionally declaim lyrically in shorter meters. Since the dramatic action is rather slight, the appeal of the recitation must have lain mainly in its lyrical passages.

All roles were undoubtedly played by boys, but one may hope that for that of Judith, some form of feminine costume was allowed. The costumes and stage setting may even have been elaborate, but we may be sure that the performance was a sedate one, suited not only for clerics and strictly educated youths, but also for the pious young queen.

On November 18, she and the archduke departed to continue their journey across Italy. The grandest receptions and entertainments were in Mantua, where Duke Vincenzo had arranged an extremely lavish production of Battista Guarini's pastoral play, the *Pastor fido*,[96] in Milan, in Pavia, and in Genoa, where, on February 18 the two parties took ship for Spain.

After the departure of Margaret and her cousin, Clement prepared to return to Rome. The *Corpus Domini*, in the care of Angelo Rocca, once again preceded him. After taking an emotional leave of Ferrarese officials, the pope set out on November 26.[97] This time, he passed through the great papal city of Bologna, making a grand entry whose *apparati* have been preserved in unusually handsome engravings published with the *livret*.[98] He arrived in Rome on December 19, warmly greeted by the populace, who had grown unaccustomed to having their prince stay away for so long.[99]

The Themes of the Entries

Of the five Ferrarese entries in 1598, only three, those of the cardinal, the pope, and the queen, have left us a good description of *apparati* and the texts of inscriptions. The two dukes were not greeted with elaborate decorations in the streets, and the whole splendor of those occasions lay in the brilliance of the costumes and magnificence of the processions. The *apparati* for the cardinal, including triumphal arches, had not been finished, less for lack of time than because of persistent rain, a natural condition that really does make outdoor construction with temporary material virtually impossible. The rather brief descriptions in the printed *livret* and the similar ones in the manuscript *Annali* of Filippo Rodi[100] give us, however, at least a glimpse of the thematic plan, however imperfectly it may have been realized. The three arches or *portoni* were, as has been noted, dedicated to abstract qualities: Glory, Immortality, and Felicity. The inscriptions and iconography of the first two aim mainly at praising the pope and his nephew the cardinal, who are hailed both as military victors and as holy peacemakers. The third arch looks forward hopefully to a period of peace and prosperity. The allusions to clemency, in the iconography of the gate decoration and of this arch, were not only a tasteful evocation of the pontiff's name, but also an expression of the general hope that the new rulers would not hold earlier support of Cesare d'Este against the *comune* and the population. (And in fact, Clement and his legate showed themselves to be quite forgiving.)

The combination of religious and military, or other secular motifs was to recur in the entry of Pope Clement himself. The precedent for such a thing went back at least to the time of Julius II, the warrior pope who had reconquered Bologna for the States of the Church in 1506. On his entry into that city on November 11, he had been hailed as a classical *triumphator* as well as Holy Father. One inscription saluted him as both "Giver of the City's Liberty" and "Restorer of the Ecclesiastical State," two qualifications the city's republicans doubtless found to be incompatible. The promiscuity of pagan and Christian themes was even more striking in Julius's return to Rome from that victorious northern campaign. His entry into the *Urbs* took place on Palm Sunday, March 28, 1507, and its decorations mingled evocations of Christ's humble entry into Jerusalem with the *triumphus* of a victorious Roman general. There were both triumphal arches and a triumphal chariot,[101] but churches along the entry route from the Porta del Popolo to Saint Peter's had outside altars in commemoration of the Christian holiday. Inscriptions greeted the pope classically as "Divus Julius," and as "Expeller of Tyrants," and one arch echoed an earlier Julius's "veni, vidi, vici."[102]

That, however, had been the High Renaissance; the same easy promiscuity of pagan and Christian themes was no longer possible in the full

Counter-Reformation. Already in 1571 Pope Pius V had objected to what seemed an excessively pagan tone in plans for the Roman triumph of Marc'Antonio Colonna, one of the victorious generals at Lepanto.[103] Some motifs of temporal conquest were inevitable in 1598, but there was little to offend the pious. The inscription at the *porta* hailing at least the papal nephew for a "war felicitously waged," was in company with an affected pleasantry about the city's opening its gates to him who opens those of heaven. The inscription of the second arch alluded to the "most glorious, almost divine" victory that Clement had obtained "without blood, without fraud." The imitation of Trajan's column had statues of Saint Peter and Saint Paul at its base, but constituted only a mild, inoffensive combination of the classical and Christian traditions,[104] and the inscription's remark about Clement's fame being inscribed in the hearts of men rather than in stone was quite unobjectionable. The "Golden Peace" promised by the inscription at Canto del Saracino (like the "serenity" foreseen in the third arch erected for the cardinal) was analogous to the return of a golden age that Renaissance flattery commonly predicted after a foreign conquest.

Another indication of the change of spirit since the High Renaissance can be seen in the numerous personifications and other portrayals of abstract qualities, such as the Glory, Immortality, and Felicity to which the cardinal's three arches had been dedicated, or the "Gloria Aldobrandina" figured in an image of the reconstruction of Trajan's Column for Clement, or the personified Religion and Justice of the queen's entry. Such personifications and portrayals are to some degree reminiscent of medieval allegory, but they are related more particularly to the vogue of emblematics, a vogue which had greatly prospered since the early cinquecento, and now appears to us as one of the essential characteristics of the baroque spirit. It was no longer in good taste to compare a pope to a conquering Roman general, but the glory of his family could be exalted in what was thought to be a classical way. Classical forms remained, but the messages they conveyed were often different.

The "prospect" or arch erected for the pope at the Porta Montagna was more original and more interesting than the others because of its use of classical conceits to present a quite timely and concrete request to the new ruler of the city. The god representing the river Po, a bearded old man leaning on an urn, is a commonplace figure for Renaissance triumphal *apparati*, in which river deities often stood for whole provinces or countries. What is remarkable is that here the Po is the father of the maiden representing Ferrara—and his urn is dry; he is *exanimus*, "lifeless." The branch of the Po flowing by Ferrara, and splitting south of the city into the Po di Volano and the Po di Primaro, today essentially a dead stream, was already silting up at the end of the sixteenth century, and the city's commerce was suffering badly. In the entry *apparato*, the citizens seem to be asking Clement to undertake engineering works to revive the stream: ". . . illi da fundere linphas": "let him flow with waters." In fact, there was much discussion about this problem during the pope's stay, with the architect and engineer G. B. Aleotti, whom we have noted as the future architect of the Teatro Farnese in Parma, being a principal consultant.[105] Although he is remembered mainly for his designs of theaters and theatrical sets for the Este, Gonzaga, and Farnese, Aleotti was, like Michelangelo, as much at home with civil engineering projects as with artistic ones. He had served Duke Alfonso in a number of practical enterprises, and was to do the same for the papal government. Beginning in 1604, that government commissioned several hydraulic projects to aid navigation and prevent floods. The branch of the Po passing by the city walls does not seem ever to have become really navigable again, despite the work, but a canal to the main channel of the Po was eventually constructed.[106]

If the above interpretation of the *apparato* with the classical river god is correct, then Ferrara was giving the pope a message very similar to that tendered in 1515 to Charles of Austria, the future Charles V, on his entry into Bruges.[107] The commercial prosperity of the Flemish city had been declining rapidly, partly as a result of the silting up of the Zwyn river. The city fathers who planned the pageantry hoped both for engineering projects and for laws more favorable to commerce. One street construction showed the maiden Bruges in a piteous state of weakness, clad in poor raiment, and seated on a throne of iron, after having occupied a golden one in the days of her prosperity. The allegorical characters *Negoce* and *Marchandise* were seen fleeing from her.[108] In the Renaissance, poetic conceits and mythological allusions could give elegance and rhetorical force to completely practical messages.

In the entry of Margaret and Albert of Austria, the *apparati* inside and outside the city gate and the other grand one at the entrance to the courtyard of the Castello had three predictable main themes: Religion, Holy Marriage, and the Glory of the House of Austria. The awe with which Italy and the rest of southern Europe regarded the Habsburgs is without parallel today. Neither the partial dissipation of their tremendous power with the separation of the Spanish and imperial thrones on the death of Charles V in mid-century, nor the more recent defeat of the Spanish Armada, had much diminished the Italian dependence upon the good will of Habsburg rulers. The kingdom of Naples and the duchy of Milan were under direct Spanish rule, while the republic of Genoa and the duchy of Mantua were more or less Spanish vassals. Venice maintained its independence only by exercising prudence. As for the popes, they too had to be careful, and in 1595 Clement had shown unusual daring in recognizing the reconversion of Henry IV of France against bitter Spanish opposition. The current grand duke of Tuscany, Ferdinand I de' Medici, had shown similar independence in 1589 by marrying a French princess, breaking thereby with the exclusively Spanish allegiance of his brother Francesco and his father Cosimo I. In 1600 he was also to betroth his niece Maria de' Medici to French king Henry IV. Such stirrings of independence amounted, however, to scarcely more than a playing of the French against the Spanish. The Habsburg family, whose ancestral *imperatores* and *Reyes Católicos* are evoked in the inscription at the Castello, were the powers that be for most Italians of 1598.

As for the *Pietas* of the queen, alluded to at the gate and at the Castello, it was in this case, unlike some others, scarcely exaggerated. We have noted that Margaret declined to dance after her marriage because she had taken communion. In Ferrara as in the other cities visited, she sought out holy relics. On the evening of Monday the sixteenth, she and Albert went to a convent in order to see a vial of the miraculous blood of Christ, continuing on to another convent later for a concert of sacred music. As a faithful servant of the Church, Margaret could be accounted a worthy recipient of the Golden Rose.

The Cavalier Reale describes in his *livret* an additional *apparato* for the royal entry, commissioned not by the pope or by the city fathers, but by the Spanish ambassador to the Holy See, the duke of Sessa. It consisted mainly of a large *chiaroscuro* painting on the façade of his temporary residence, the Palazzo dei Diamanti, which lay on the entry route from the gate to the Castello. Under the arms of the pope, the emperor, king of Spain, and Margaret, the painting had two female figures representing Religion and Justice. A third lady, standing for Victory, was descending from Heaven and pointing to the arms. The inscription was "Foelicitas Soeculi." There could scarcely have been a more pointed or succinct expression of the Habsburg view of European affairs. Salvation and prosperity lay in the hands of the Empire and of Spain, allied with the Holy Catholic Church.

The Livrets *and Their Authors*

The various named and anonymous authors of the *livrets* for the Ferrara entries may be divided into three main categories: courtiers, journalists, and officials. In the first group must be placed Vincenzo Greco and Antonio da Ischia, the two southern Italians who wrote flattering reports of the entry of Duke Ranuccio Farnese. The Cavalier Reale, whose account of Margaret's entry appeared in Ferrara itself, probably wished for reward both from the royal party and from the papal court.

The case of the unnamed author of the description of the pope's entry that we reproduce, *La felice entrata*, is somewhat different but not unrelated. One can almost certainly identify him as Filippo Rodi, Ferrarese doctor of law and author of the manuscript chronicle called *Annali*, cited here several times for events during 1597–1598. The wording of his account of the papal entry in the *Annali* is often identical to that of the printed *livret* (with the manuscript version being very slightly fuller). It is not impossible that he was also the author of the anonymous *livret* for the departure of Cesare and entry of the cardinal, for its content is very close to that of the account in the *Annali*. Here, however, there is enough difference of wording to leave some doubt. A natural suspicion that the annalist may have copied the two *livrets* is largely invalidated when we note that the style is perfectly in keeping with that found throughout the long chronicle, which includes numerous accounts of events of pageantry and Este fêtes.

Rodi's *Annali*, which begin with the origins of Ferrara, may be divided into two parts, the first being a history of the city's past drawn from various written sources; and the second, starting with the author's young adulthood, being first-hand, or near first-hand, accounts of contemporary events. As early as 1560 Rodi was describing the entry of Lucrezia de' Medici, first bride of Duke Alfonso II.[109] He also recounted those of the second and third brides, Barbara d'Austria and Margherita Gonzaga, as well as a number of less official celebrations. His *Annali* break off, as we noted earlier, during the summer of 1598, after the entries of the cardinal, pope, and duke of Mantua, but before those of the duke of Parma and the queen. The work ends with some descriptions of changes made by the pope in the Ferrarese government and laws. If one judges from the dates of his first apparently eye-witness descriptions, Rodi must in 1598 have been quite old; and it seems likely that he may have become unable to continue his annals. He was, in sum, also a courtier of a sort, but one of considerable standing and seriousness. As a doctor of law, he may well, for example, have been one of the honored citizens who carried the poles of the papal *baldacchino*, if his health permitted. Just as importantly for his attitude and motives, he was a local historian, devoted to the life of his city, rather than just to a particular patron.

The case of the lawyer Giovan Battista Grillo, whose narration of the queen's whole journey appeared only six years after the events, is also interesting.[110] He was a Neapolitan, and thus a subject of the king of Spain. Finding himself in Mantua on business when the queen's imminent Italian journey was announced, he apparently conceived the idea of writing a general account of her Italian progress and presenting it to Spanish rulers at home. He was not present on the earliest part of Margaret's journey, and probably not in Ferrara either, but he clearly drew on the *livrets* published at the time, and no doubt also on first-hand reports. He was on the spot in Mantua and has left us a most detailed and interesting description of the production of Guarini's *Pastor fido* before the queen. He then accompanied the royal party as far as Milan, but informs the reader that he fell ill there and was unable to go on to Genoa. The illness perhaps explains the long delay in the publication of his work, which appeared in Naples in 1604, dedicated to the Spanish viceroy.

The Annibale Banordini who "gathered" information about the entry of the pope to send it to Rome, and the Geronimo Amarotti who did the same for the entries of the Venetians and Vincenzo Gonzaga, may, on the other hand, have been in the pay of the publisher Bonfadino, who was a sort of specialist in bringing out news bulletins.[111] Indeed, we cannot be sure they were in Ferrara at all; they may simply have edited reports arriving in Rome. That was certainly the role of Bernardo Beccari, who "published" accounts of the queen's entry and *sposalizio*. Numerous other news bulletins of his confection have survived, and more must have been lost. He was not unlike a modern newspaper editor who puts together information from distant correspondents.

It is into the third, most learned category that we must place the two papal officials Angelo Rocca (1545–1620) and Giovan Paolo Mocante (d. 1617). The first is not, strictly speaking, the author of a *livret*, for he was in no great hurry to get his narrative out, and writing in Latin cut him off from the masses of secular readers reached by the other authors. With scholarly unconcern for journalistic appeal, he set the account into the framework of a treatise on a broader subject, although there is no doubt that the treatise itself was inspired by the events he describes. Rocca was an authority of considerable standing in the Church, having gone on from a doctorate in theology earned at Padua to be the head of the Vatican printing house and a principal editor of the Vulgate Bible.[112] He wrote treatises on a variety of subjects, from sacred ritual to games of cards and dice (of which he disapproved). He was also a bibliophile, and his personal collection of books forms the nucleus of the Roman library that still bears his name, the Angeli-ca, frequented today by scholars of sixteenth- and seventeenth-century subjects. Something of Rocca's personality and sense of his high position comes through in the accounts of his travel with the *Corpus Domini*, and in the proud figure he cuts in the engravings.

In 1602, three years after the original publication, parts of Rocca's account of the papal entry reappeared in a mysterious, and certainly unauthorized, new edition.[113] These passages were reproduced faithful-ly, but were preceded by a short consolation to Christian princes who had had their rightful possessions taken away by Roman pontiffs (3–14), and followed by *exempla* of great rulers of the past who are recorded as having made *modest* entries into conquered cities. Some speculation about the identity of the anonymous, anti-papal publishers can be found in Appendix II to this introduction.

Less is known about the life of Master of Ceremonies Giovan Paolo Mocante than about that of Rocca, but he too had a good position at the papal court, and was already an established chronicler of ec-clesiastical travel and ceremonies.[114] He was ordained and had fol-lowed the examples of a grandfather and an older brother in becoming a papal master of ceremonies in 1592. The grandfather, Biagio da Cesena, had had the major role in planning the ritual for the papal coronation of the emperor Charles V at Bologna in 1530.[115] We may speculate that the brother, Francesco, was probably responsible for obtaining Giovan Paolo his position in the Vatican. In 1595, as third master of ceremonies, the latter had published an account of Pope Clement's ab-

solution of Henry IV and of the subsequent processions held in Rome
to celebrate the event.[116] The next year he had accompanied Cardinal-
legate Caetani on a mission to the king of Poland, and composed a
description of the journey that the historian Pastor found to be of considerable interest and part of which has recently been edited and published by a Polish scholar.[117] After arriving in Ferrara with the pope,
in 1598, Mocante prepared for Roman publication a report of the entry of Ranuccio Farnese (described in the Bibliography) and then the
much fuller one on the entry and *sposalizio* of Margaret. He also left
a manuscript diary stretching over a number of years of his service,
which survives in several complete or partial copies. The volume cover-
ing events of 1598 that I have consulted in the Archivio di Stato, Modena, has no fewer than 903 manuscript pages.[118] Mocante was by
profession, of course, an expert in matters of form and ritual; and his
narrations of the various meetings of the pope and the queen, and
descriptions of the religious services include authoritative commentary.
He seems, however, to have been less fussy and presumptuous in character than his predecessors Johann Burchard and Paride de' Grassi, whose
Latin diaries chronicle the ceremonial activities of Popes Alexander
VI, Julius II and Leo X.[119] It is not just that Mocante was different in
personal character; he seems also to have been conscious of writing
for a larger audience, and particularly for laymen as well as for clerics.
Many merchants, and even artisans, were now purchasing news bulletins, which Bulgarelli thinks may have been printed in larger quanti-
ties than most books, despite the scarcity of surviving copies.[120]
Mocante must have understood that, although they delighted in reading of *magnificenza*, particularly that of their own lords, laymen were
not primarily interested in technical questions of ritual and precedence.
His account is unusually readable, as well as informative, and its purchasers got their money's worth.

Conclusion

For a year the inhabitants of Ferrara could almost have imagined
that with the departure of its old lords, their city had become the fo-
cal point of European politics. Certainly it seemed to be a more important capital than it had ever been. This impression was, of course,
illusory, for Ferrara would no longer be a capital at all once the pope

had gone, just a larger than average town of the Papal States. It would be governed by a cardinal-legate, subordinate to the pope and College of Cardinals in Rome, and working through the *Giudice* and the *Savi*, whose survival assured some continuity in political forms. It could no longer attract the visit of great personages, except in transit, although the local nobility, and sometimes the legate, would insure the maintenance of a very creditable level of cultural life, particularly in music and the theater.

Had the triumphal and ceremonial events of 1598 been a sham, and the spectators, dupes? Not really; or at least not on every plane. Certainly the Ferrarese, whose enthusiasm is recorded in the *livrets* and chronicles, were no more deceived than the pope and other illustrious personages who were the main actors of the pageantry; and "deception" is not really an accurate term for the context. The dignified representatives of the remarkable variety of political entities that came together in one year at one place were all bent upon the universal purpose of civic pageantry, which is to present an image of the majesty of the state. It is important to note, too, that all received as well as gave civic messages.

The first protagonists were the cardinal and pope on the one hand, and the representatives of the *comune*—that is, the *Giudice* and the *Savi* and the costumed companies of well-born young Ferrarese—on the other. The townsmen were intent upon informing the pontiff of the local government's vigor and reliability after centuries of princely rule, while Clement wished, after conquest, to assure the inhabitants of his benevolence and fairmindedness. He wanted also for them to see how grand and august was the political structure of which they were now to be a part. The blending of civic and religious motifs, as when the *Corpus Domini* preceded the conqueror into the city, amounted virtually to an identification of the state with the church. It was an identification with which the citizens of Rome and neighboring Bologna were already familiar, and which would eventually seem normal to most Ferrarese. The citizens also seized the occasion, as we have seen, to make a practical request of the pope, and it was certainly understood. He might have replied in the words supposedly spoken by Queen Elizabeth I on the occasion of her 1559 entry into London: "I have taken notice of your good meaning unto me, and will endeavor to Answere your severall expectations."[121]

The two dukes and the Venetians wished to impress both Clement and the citizenry (although certainly more the former than the latter) with their power and *magnificenza*, and they wanted also to communicate their friendly acceptance of an altered political situation. For his part, the pontiff first desired all to see that he was now in firm control of the former duchy, and then that he forgave all past open or tacit support for the cause of Cesare d'Este. The Habsburgs, arriving later, were probably too sure of their family's position to think much of impressing Italians with its power, but they wanted Clement to know of their personal devotion to the Church, which certainly seems to have been genuine. On his side, the pope must have been glad of a chance to show favor to the bride of Philip III after quarreling with the prince's father over the absolution of Henry IV. He had not given up the Spanish alliance for a French one, but intended to promote a balance of power between the *Rey Católico* and the *Roy Treschrestien*, hoping for the support of both against the Protestants and the Turks.

We may assume that all these messages were received, and that all parties concerned were to some degree placed under obligation by the ritual and dramatic dialogues in which they had participated. But pageantry was not entirely a matter of political communication; it was also a theatrical experience, both for the spectators and for the participants. To adapt an Aristotelian term, one might say that it afforded a sort of catharsis of the political emotions. The most skeptical and worldly-wise of participants and observers were likely to be carried away by the spirit of the occasion, and it would be excessively cynical on the part of later historians to assume that no lasting benefit came from the experience, whatever discouraging events may have followed. If men were supposed to be made morally better by the catharsis of pity and fear in tragedy, some lingering political edification may well have come too from the theater of well-staged civic pageantry.

Notes

1. Such are, for example, the account of King Francis I's 1515 entry into Lyon, MS. Extravagantes 86.4 at the Herzog August Bibliothek in Wolfenbüttel, and, from that same year, a report of Prince Charles of Habsburg's entry into Bruges, now MS. 2591 of the Oesterreichische Nationalbibliothek, Vienna.

2. Many reports on events of pageantry sent home to the Venetian government can be found in *I diarii di Marino Sanuto (MCCCCXCVI–MDXXXIII)*, ed. Renato Fulin et al. (Venice: F. Visentini, 1879–1913), 58 vols., and many more remain in manuscript at the Archivio di Stato in Venice. Some pageantry accounts can be found also in a set of manuscript *avvisi* sent to the Fugger firm in Augs-

burg during the second half of the century that found its way into the Vatican's Urbinas collection, alongside an equally important set of *avvisi* sent to the dukes of Urbino. See René Ancel, "Étude critique sur quelques recueils d'*avvisi*: contribution à l'histoire du journalisme en Italie," *Mélanges d'Archéologie et d'Histoire de l'École Française de Rome*, XXVIIIe année (1908): 117–139.

3. The anonymous *Ordine de le noze de lo Illustrissimo Signor Misir Constantio Sfortia de Aragonia: et de la Ilustrissima Madona Camilla de Aragonia sua consorte nel anno 1475 a di infrascripto* (Vicentie [Vicenza]: Hermano Levilapide, 1475) [BNP, BLL].

4. *Ingressus Xtianissimi Ludovici Francorum Regis in civitatem suam Mediolan.* (N.p.: n.pub., 1499) [BNP].

5. Anonymous, *La festa che si fece in Siena a di. xv. dagho. M.D.VI.* (N.p.: n.pub., n.d., but doubtless Siena, 1506) [Arsenal].

6. Gian Giacomo Penna, *Cronica delle magnifiche et honorate pompe fatte in Roma per la creatione et incoronatione di Papa Leone. X. Pont. Opt. Max.* (N.p.: n.pub., n.d., but probably Florence, 1513) [BNCF].

7. Later printed by A. Ademollo as "Magnifica et sumptuosa festa facta dalli S. R. per il carnovale M.D.XIII," in *Alessandro VI, Giulio II e Leone X nel carnevale di Roma, documenti inediti* (Florence: C. Ademollo, 1886), 35–70.

8. See Fabrizio Cruciani's edition and study, *Il teatro del Campidoglio e le feste romane del 1513, con la ricostruzione architettonica del teatro di Arnaldo Bruschi* (Milan: Il Polifilo, 1968).

9. See Giovanni Alberto Albicante, *Trattato del'intrar in Milano di Carlo V.C. sempre Aug. con le proprie figure de li archi, e per ordine, li nobili vassalli e prencipi e signori cesarei* . . . (Milan: Andrea Calvi, 1541) [BNCF].

10. A certain number of these, say 20 or 25, may have been excluded by Bulgarelli as being too literary, but the majority meet his criteria.

11. All the identified authors of *livrets* with which I am familiar were men, with the single exception of the Bolognese woman Gratia Masolini, who did one of the bulletins reporting on Pope Clement's progress to Ferrara listed in note 54.

12. See Guido Mazenta, *Apparato fatto dalla città di Milano per ricevere la Serenissima Regina D. Margarita d'Austria sposata al Potentiss. Rè di Spagna D. Filippo III. nostro signore* (Milan: Pacifico Pontio, 1599) [BLL]. Mazenta's analysis of the *apparati* is particularly good, although he apologizes for having had to rush into print without time to include drawings or to compose his description in Latin. He notes that the first part of the text, with description of the decorations, was done five days before the event, with the account of the actual entry being added later.

13. See, for example, Pierfrancesco Giambullari, *Apparato et feste nelle noze del Illustrissimo Signor Duca di Firenze, Et della Duchessa sua consorte, con le stanze, madriali, comedia, et intermedii in quelle recitate* (Florence: Benedetto Giunta, 1539) [BNCF]. In an even rarer occurrence, the special music written for this occasion was also printed, in a separate publication: anonymous editor, *Musiche fatte nelle nozze dello Illustrissimo Duca di Firenze il Signor Cosimo de' Medici et della illustrissima consorte sua Mad. Leonora di Tolleto* (Venice: A. Gardane, 1539) [Oesterreichische Nationalbibliothek, Vienna].

14. "Essai de critique interne des livres d'entrées français du XVIe siècle," in Jean Jacquot, ed., *Les Fêtes de la Renaissance III* (Paris: Centre National de la

Introduction

Recherche Scientifique, 1975), 187–200. Françoise Decroisette, a participant at that 1972 colloquium, recently addressed some of the same concerns in a most interesting way at another French festival colloquium. See her "Perception, espace, temps dans les récits de l'entrée de Charles Quint à Bologne en 1530," in the anonymously edited *La Fête et l'écriture: théâtre de cour, cour-théâtre en Espagne et en Italie, 1450–1530*, Colloque International France-Espagne-Italie, Aix-en-Provence, 6–7–8 décembre 1985, Études Hispano-Italiennes, 1 (Aix-en-Provence: Publications-Diffusion Université de Provence, 1987), 303–319.

15. Paolo Palliolo, in Cruciani, *Il teatro del Campidoglio*, 33–34.

16. See Publio Fontana, *Il sontuoso apparato fatta dalla magnifica città di Brescia nel felice ritorno dell'Illus. & Reverendiss. vescovo suo il Cardinale Morosini. Con la spositione de' sensi simbolici che in esso si contengono.* (Brescia: Vincenzo Sabbio, 1591) [Herzog August Bibliothek, Wolfenbüttel].

17. See, among other studies, Mona Ozouf, *La Fête révolutionnaire* (Paris: Gallimard, 1976).

18. An over-all picture of the Este as patrons of letters can be had from Edmund G. Gardner's now somewhat dated *Dukes and Poets in Ferrara: A Study in the Poetry, Religion and Politics of the Fifteenth and Early Sixteenth Centuries* (New York: E. P. Dutton & Co., n.d.). More recent assessments of both literary and artistic patronage can be found in various essays of *La corte e lo spazio: Ferrara estense*, ed. Giuseppe Papagno and Amedeo Quondam, 3 vols. (Rome: Bulzoni, 1982), while in *Ferrara: The Style of a Renaissance Despotism* (Princeton Univ. Press, 1973), Werner L. Gundersheimer provides analyses of Este cultural policies in various areas during the quattrocento.

19. See Lewis Lockwood's *Music in Renaissance Ferrara 1400–1505: The Creation of a Musical Center in the Fifteenth Century* (Cambridge, MA: Harvard Univ. Press, 1984), and also his article "Ferrara" in the *New Grove's Dictionary of Music and Musicians*, ed. Stanley Sadie (London: Macmillan, 1980). Interesting information about the numerous musicians on the payroll of Ercole I in 1476 is given by Gundersheimer in *Ferrara: The Style of a Renaissance Despotism*, 294–95.

20. Charles M. Rosenberg examines early Este policies in regard to the San Giorgio and three other annual festivals in "The Use of Celebrations in Public and Semi-Public Affairs in Fifteenth-Century Ferrara," published in Maristella Panizza de Lorch, ed., *Il teatro italiano del Rinascimento* (Milan: Edizioni di Communità, 1980), 521–35.

21. On this general subject, see Giovanni Carandente, *I trionfi nel primo Rinascimento* (Turin: Edizioni Radiodiffusione Italiana, 1963), which deals with actual triumphal processions as well as with many portrayals of triumphs in the figurative arts.

22. See the anonymous *Diario ferrarese*, edited by Giuseppe Pardi in *RIS*, tomo 24, parte 7, vol. 1, pp. 35–36. Borso's investiture is recounted also in Frate Giovanni Ferrarese's Latin chronicle *Ex Annalium Marchionum Estensium Excerpta*, ed. Luigi Simeoni, *RIS*, tomo 21, parte 2, pp. 39–40.

23. Frate Giovanni Ferrarese describes the two entries in the *Excerpta*, 41–47. For Reggio, see as well the special account of Malatesta Ariosti published by Adolfo Levi as *L'ingresso di Borso d'Este a Reggio nel 1453*, Per le Nozze Levi-Sottocasa (Reggio, 1899).

24. Published by E. Celani in "La venuta di Borso d'Este in Roma," *Archivio della R. Società Romana di Storia Patria* 13 (1890): 362–450.

25. "La venuta," (note 24 above), 405.

26. See Appendix I for a compilation of the principal Ferrarese entries from the death of Borso in 1471 to the devolution of 1598, with indications of contemporary sources.

27. Much about the distinguished cultural history of Alfonso's reign can be learned from Angelo Solerti's long introduction to his edition of Annibale Romei's discourses in *Ferrara e la corte estense nella seconda metà del secolo decimosesto*. . . . (Città di Castello: S. Lapi, 1891).

28. Among several published accounts of Johanna's Florentine entry, the principal is Domenico Mellini's *Descrizione dell'entrata della Sereniss. Reina Giovanna d'Austria et dell'apparato fatto in Firenze*. . . . (Florence: Giunti, 1566) [BNCF]. For the later entertainments Mellini also did a *Descrizione dell'apparato della commedia et intermedii d'essa recitata in Firenze*. . . . (Florence: Giunti, 1566) [Moren.].

29. The anonymously published *Narratione* (more fully described in Appendix I) describes the various courtly entertainments only briefly and does not give the title of the *torneo*, which is known from other sources. The entertainments have been studied by Irène Mamczarz in "Une Fête équestre à Ferrare: Il tempio d'amore (1565)," in Jean Jacquot, ed., *Les Fêtes de la Renaissance* III (Paris: Centre National de la Recherche Scientifique, 1975), 349–72. Her study, based in large part on an account in the manuscript *Annali* of Filippo Rodi, is particularly interesting for information on the contributions of Tasso.

30. A concise survey of theatrical history in Ferrara, with many titles and dates, can be found in Elena Povoledo's article "Ferrara" for the *Enciclopedia dello spettacolo* (Rome: Le Maschere, 1954–67). The organization of the following discussion, and most of its interpretations, are, however, my own.

31. Much information about their activities can be found in Anthony Newcomb, *The Madrigal at Ferrara 1579–1597*, 2 vols. (Princeton Univ. Press, 1980).

32. See Elena Povoledo's article "Torneo" in the *Enciclopedia dello spettacolo*.

33. All these tourneys are the subject of a recent general study by Guido Baldassari, "Cavallerie della città di Ferrara," in the new scholarly review founded by the Istituto di Studi Rinascimentali, Ferrara: *Schifanoia* 1 (1987): 100–126. Baldassari's essay, which endeavors to suggest new directions for research, is particularly rich in bibliographical references.

34. See Margaret M. McGowan, *L'Art du ballet de cour en France 1581–1643* (Paris: Éditions du Centre National de la Recherche Scientifique, 1963).

35. For the character and tastes of Margherita and her two predecessors, see Alfonso Lazzari, *Le ultime tre duchesse di Ferrara e la corte estense ai tempi di Torquato Tasso* (Rovigo: Società Tipografica Editrice Rodigino, 1952).

36. The book had the title *Banchetti, compositioni di vivande* in its first printing (Ferrara: G. de Buglhat & A. Hucher, 1549) [BNCF], and was called *Libro novo nel qual s'insegna à far d'ogni sorte di vivanda* for later Venetian editions. In one section the author tells of an elaborate banquet, with a playing of Ariosto's *La Cassaria*, that was given in honor of Duke Alfonso I by his heir Ercole in 1529.

37. Among other things he "scooped" the Venetians by having the Gelosi troop of actors, whom they had engaged to perform for Henry, give an earlier private performance before the king and himself. Much information on the duke's behavior during Henry's progress across Italy is given in Pierre de Nolhac and Angelo Solerti's *Il viaggio in Italia di Enrico III re di Francia*. . . . (Turin: L. Roux, 1890).

Introduction

38. Ferdinando de' Medici had given up his cardinal's hat in order to marry after succeeding his brother Francesco as grand duke of Tuscany in 1587, and Archduke Albert of Austria did the same to marry the Spanish infanta in 1598, but such actions were unusual.

39. The most detailed history of the complex political events by which Ferrara did in fact devolve to the Church, from the moment of Pius V's Bull to that of Clement VIII's arrival in the city, is E. Callegari, "La devoluzione di Ferrara alla Santa Sede (1598) da documenti inediti degli Archivi di Stato di Modena e Venezia," *Rivista Storica Italiana* 12 (1895): 1–57. Writing not long after the Risorgimento, Callegari takes a pronounced anti-papal stance. A view more favorable to Clement was put forward three years later by Virginio Prinzivalli in "La devoluzione di Ferrara alla S. Sede secondo una relazione inedita di Camillo Capilupi," *Atti della Deputazione Ferrarese di Storia Patria*, prima serie, 10 (1898): 121–333. The near-contemporary account which Prinzivalli published (139–302) was that of a Mantuan cleric living in Rome who had served in Vatican diplomacy and was experienced at writing treatises on contemporary political events. It is most interesting for the accounts of diplomatic maneuvers in Rome, and less so for events in Ferrara. My summary of events is taken principally from these two sources. Additional ones are indicated in the course of the summary.

40. L. M. Muratori, writing two centuries after the birth, and striving to please a descendant who was the current duke of Modena and Reggio, devoted more than eighty pages of his *Delle antichità estensi* ([Modena: Nella Stamperia Ducale, 1740], 2: 422–505) to arguments in support of the legitimacy of Cesare's descent.

41. This ritual homage to democracy and republicanism in a hereditary principality is said to have greatly irritated Pope Clement when it was alleged as a proof of the legitimacy of Cesare's succession. As a feudal lord, the pontiff was no more interested than his secular colleagues in encouraging the idea of popular sovereignty. See Pastor, *History of the Popes*, 24: 387–88. A very good account of events in Ferrara from the moment of Alfonso's death through the devolution and the grand civic occasions of 1598 can be found in Faustini, 103–182. That seventeenth-century author had access to numerous recent archival records, as well, apparently, as to some of the *livrets* reproduced in this edition. He also knew older people who had participated in the events of 1598, and seems to have recalled witnessing them himself as a child. His accounts contain interesting details and anecdotes. Shorter recollections of the same events may be found in the memoirs of Cardinal Guido Bentivoglio, a Ferrarese of noble family who had been a very young cleric at the time. Bentivoglio had hastened to transfer his loyalty to the new regime, and the pope's favorable acceptance of his overtures had marked the beginning of a distinguished career in ecclesiastical diplomacy. See his *Memorie e lettere*, ed. Costantino Panigada, Scrittori d'Italia, 150 (Bari: Gius. Laterza, 1934), 8–25. The manuscript diaries and chronicles cited in my bibliography also have accounts of events between Alfonso's death and the devolution. Particularly interesting descriptions of Cesare's investiture are given by Rodi, *Annali* IV, fols. 208^r–209^v; and Guarini, *Diario* I, fols. 124^r–126^r. My account of events in the city during these months is taken from Faustini unless another source is indicated.

42. The following summary of diplomatic attitudes and maneuvers is derived mainly from the studies of Callegari and Prinzivalli, cited in note 39 above.

43. For the negotiations, December 31, 1597, to January 13, 1598, and also

for events in Ferrara during that fortnight, see Luigi Balduzzi, "L'istrumento finale della transazione di Faenza pel passaggio di Ferrara dagli Estensi alla S. Sede (13 gennaio 1598)," *Atti e Memorie della R. Deputazione di Storia Patria per le Provincie di Romagna*, terza serie, 9 (1891): 80–110.

44. See Callegari, 39–41.

45. His continuation of Sardi's *Historie ferraresi*, 140.

46. See Faustini, 138–140. A great grandson of the poet Ludovico Ariosto was chosen by the minor nobles as their spokesman.

47. The accounts are in A.S.Fe.: No. 17, Libro 30, of the Archivio del Comune, Serie Patriarcale. (Searchers should not be misled by the catalog description, which does not mention them.) Faccini is the only artist named who can be surely identified in the Thieme-Becker *Künstler Lexikon* (Leipzig: Wilhelm Engelmann, then E. A. Seemann, 1907–1950). Giovan Battista da Tamara may be the same as the *Lexikon*'s Giovan Battista da Ferrara, known to have been working in the region about this time. Other artists reported as having received payments were Giulio Milanese, Antonio Bonzo, and Gaspare Mignelli. The spellings for the surnames of the last two are doubtful.

48. *Annali* IV, fols. 273ʳ–278ʳ. The only other manuscript diary with a fairly full account of the entry is Guarini's *Diario* II, fols. 2ʳ–4ʳ.

49. This story is told most fully by Faustini, 146 and 150. The cardinal is said to have paid a ransom for the horse several days later.

50. For these events, see Faustini, 147–50.

51. For the reception of the envoys in Rome, see Faustini, 153–54.

52. See Pastor, 24: 396–97.

53. *Ordine et cerimonie della partenza del Santissimo Sacramento di Roma. Et nell'entrare nelle città, terre ò luoghi dove si haverà da fermare, ò posare la notte. Et della partita di Sua Santita da Roma, & dell'entrata semplice che farà nelle città terre, luoghi, ò castelli per tutto il viaggio dove si fermerà, ò la mattina à pranso, ò la sera a dormire.* In Roma, in Bologna & in Ferrara, et ristampata in Padova: Appresso Lorenzo Pasquati, 1598 [Vat.].

54. The most important of these *livrets* are: Gratia Masolini, *Narratione dell'accoglienze fatte da molte città alla Santità di N. Signore Papa Clemente VIII. Nel viaggio che ha fatto da Roma per Ferrara* (Rome: Presso Bartolomeo Bonfadino, 1598) [Vat., BLL]; and Odoardo Magliani, *Ordini tenuti nell'andata del Santissimo Sacramento e di N. S. Papa Clemente VIII. di Roma per Ferrara* (Rome: Presso Bartolomeo, 1598) [Ang]. There is another account of the pope's reception just in the cities of the duchy of Urbino: Annibal Mereggia, *Narratione dell'accoglienze fatte dal Serenissimo Duca d'Urbino. Alla Santita di N. Signore Papa Clemente VIII. . . .* (Rome: Per Bartolomeo Bonfadino, 1598) [Ang.]. The anonymous *livret* for the papal entry into Ferrara that we reproduce here also has a short recapitulation of the preceding journey.

55. The monastery has now almost completely disappeared, and the church is a baroque construction. The only significant architectural vestige from 1598 is the Renaissance campanile, designed by the talented and prolific local artist Biagio Rossetti.

56. *De Sacro Sancto Christi Corpore, Romanis Pontificibus Iter Conficientibus Praeferendo Commentarius. Antiquissimi Ritus Causam et Originem, Variasque Summorum Pontificum Sacratissimam Secum Hostiam in Itinere Deferentium Profectiones,*

Itinerarium Societatis Sanctissimi Sacramenti Clemente VIII. Pont. Max. Ferrariiam Profiscente, Eiusdemque Pontificis Solemnem in eam Civitatem Ingressum, et in Urbem Romanam Reditum Complectens. (Romae: Guillelmum Facciottum, 1599) [Columbia, BLL, Ariostea].

57. A detailed account of the entry from the papal point of view, with special attention to ceremony, is found in Mocantius's *Diarium*, 321–60. The account in Rodi's *Annali* IV, fols. 298ᵛ–303ʳ, is so similar to the printed *livret* as to make it seem likely he was the author of that anonymously published work too. See also Guarini's *Diario* II, fols. 17ᵛ–24ᵛ; and Elia Minerbi's *Memorie*, (described in Bibliography), fols. 93ʳ–93ᵛ.

58. Faustini specifies (157) that the *baldacchino* was carried first by *Savi*, then by magistrates and judges, then by *legisti*, then by medical doctors, and finally by notaries. The honor was thus shared.

59. His continuation of Sardi's *Historie ferraresi*, 163.

60. A.S.Fe.: Libro 30, no. 53, of the Archivio del Comune, Serie Patriarcale.

61. Names mentioned that are not identifiable in the *Lexikon* are: Marco Malmorino, Ercole di Vachi, Biagio Tieghi, and Gian Andrea Belloni, perhaps a relative of Giulio. The form and spellings of the surnames are not always sure.

62. The pope's pony was confiscated by Ercole Romei, one of the thirty ceremonially dressed young patricians. Faustini recounts (167–68) that in his haste to mount the animal Romei kicked the pope in the hand. Upon being told forgivingly that he could have the horse, the count took it away and offered it to a lady, who in turn gave it back to the papal household. The lady was apparently the celebrated Marfisa d'Este, whose restored *palazzina* in the Giovecca is now a museum.

63. See Faustini's account of this incident, 168–70.

64. Mucantius gives a detailed account of the ceremonies of thanksgiving in his *Diarium*, 383–89.

65. The historian Renato Fulin published some other documents from the Venetian State Archives relating to this extraordinary embassy in *Al Pontefice Clemente Ottavo ambasceria veneta straordinaria in Ferrara nell'anno MDXCVIII* (Venice: Tip. Antonelli, 1865). Good accounts of the ambassadors' entry and subsequent ceremonies are found also in Mucantius's *Diarium*, 410–12; and Guarini's *Diario* II, fols. 31ʳ–32ʳ.

66. Edward Muir has analysed the extraordinarily intricate Venetian civic ceremonial at home in *Civic Ritual in Renaissance Venice* (Princeton Univ. Press, 1981). The republic also had an unusually well-trained and sophisticated body of diplomats, adept not only at sharp negotiation, but also at what we should call "showing the flag" abroad.

67. *Public Life in Renaissance Florence* (New York: Academic Press, 1980), 287.

68. See Pastor, 24:401.

69. The following information about the Mantuan duke's entry and stay is taken essentially from the reproduced *livret*. Among the MS accounts, the fullest are those of Mucantius's *Diarium*, 410–26; Rodi's *Annali* IV, fols. 313ʳ–315ʳ; and Guarini's *Diario* II, fols. 32ʳ–33ʳ.

70. See the account of a state visit Alfonso II paid to Venice in 1562: Camillo Zio, *La solennissima entrata dell'Illustrissimo & Eccellentissimo Signor Duca di Ferrara*

ne la città di Venetia, cominciando dalla partita di Sua Eccellenza da Ferrara. . . . (Bologna: Pellegrino Bonardo, 1562) [BLL].

71. The lords of Mantua had acquired the marquisate of Monferrato through a dynastic marriage in 1536.

72. MS accounts of these celebrations are found in Minerbi's *Memorie*, fols. 98^v–99^r; and in the *Copia di cronaca anonima ferrarese dall'anno 1483 all'anno 1607* (Estense: Classe prima, MS. 641bis), under the year 1598. The leaves of the *Cronaca* are not numbered, but the year of events is indicated in the margin.

73. Cardinal Bentivoglio speculates about the duke's social insecurity and especially about the rivalry with Vincenzo Gonzaga in the *Memorie*, 17–19.

74. Bibliographical descriptions of this unreproduced *livret*, as of all others dealing with the Ferrarese events of 1598, may be found in the special bibliography at the end of this introduction. My account of Ranuccio's entry is based upon the Greco *livret* unless another source is indicated.

75. See his *Relatione* of the duke's entry (described in Bibliography), fol. A2^v.

76. In the manuscript chronicles, the best accounts of Duke Ranuccio's entry and stay in Ferrara are that of Mucantius's *Diarium*, 440–64, which is an expanded Latin version of his *livret*; and that of Guarini's *Diario* II, fols. 36^v–38^v. Rodi's narrative, which covers several decades of Ferrarese history personally experienced (as well as several centuries before the author's birth), breaks off in the summer of 1598 before the arrival of Ranuccio.

77. *Memorie*, 19.

78. For a summary of theatrical history in the city, see the article "Parma," by Angiola Maria Buonisconti and Maurizio Corradi Cervi, in the *Enciclopedia dello spettacolo*. More recent information on policies and culture in Parma during Ranuccio's time can be found in essays of *Le corti farnesiane di Parma e Piacenza, 1545–1622*, vol. 1: *Potere e società nello stato farnesiano*, ed. Marzio Achille Romani; and vol. 2: *Forme e istituzioni della produzione culturale*, ed. Amedeo Quondam (Rome: Bulzoni, 1978).

79. *Memorie*, 19–20.

80. The whole trip may be followed in a modern edition of the travel journal of Gilles Faing, a member of the archduke's household, in Louis Prosper Gachard, ed., *Collection des voyages des souverains des Pays-Bas* (Brussels: F. Hayez, 1874–82), tome 4, 478–97.

81. See Pastor, 24:402.

82. There is only one grand account of the whole Italian journey, published five years after the event: Giovanni Battista Grillo's *Breve trattato di quanto successe alla Maestà della Regina D. Margherita, N. S., dalla citta di Trento, fine d'Alemagna e principio d'Italia, sino alla città di Genova. . . .* (Naples: C. Vitale, 1604) [BLL, BNP, Genoa]. Grillo was a witness of events beginning in Mantua through those of the visit to Milan, but apparently took his information from others for the earlier and later parts of the journey. One other *livret* includes receptions in several different cities: Biagio Zerlii, *Narratione del viaggio della Serenissima Margherita d'Austria Regina di Spagna. Cominciando da Ferrara, Ostiglia, Mantova, Cremona, & Lodi, per fino a Milano. . . .* (Cremona: Barucino De Giovanni, 1599) [BNP]. Some *livrets* for individual towns and localities will be mentioned at the appropriate places in the text.

83. See the anonymous *Vera et fedele relatione del passaggio della Ser.^ma Prin-*

cipessa Margherita Regina di Spagna per lo stato de quella Serenissima Signoria di Venetia (Verona: Angelo Tano, 1599) [BNCF].

84. The *Vera et fedele relatione*, described in note 83 above, may well have been written by one of the ambassadors. Much the same ground is covered in another *livret* published also in Verona, which the royal party skirted but did not enter: Gio. Pietro Moretti, *Passaggio della Serenissima Regina Margarita d'Austria per il territorio veronese* (Verona: Angelo Tano, 1598) [BLL]. A study devoted to the history of imperial visits to the *terra ferma*, Teodoro Toderini's *Cerimoniali e feste in occasione di avvenimenti e passaggi nelli stati della repubblica veneta di duchi, arciduchi ed imperatori dell'augustissima casa d'Austria dall'anno 1361 al 1797* (Venice: Tip. di Santo Martinengo, 1857), has a little documentary material relating to this passage (43–47), although much less than might be expected given the importance of the occasion.

85. A curious anonymous *livret* recounts the governor's own journey to meet Margaret and attend her until her arrival in Milan: *Breve narratione di quanto passò appò la persona dell'Illustriss. et Eccellentiss. Signor Conestabile di Castiglia, dal giorno che partí, fino a che ritornò à Milano, con la Sereniss. et Potentiss. Regina Margherita, Signora Nostra Clementissima* (N.p.: n. pub., n.d.) [BNP]. Like that of the viceroys of Naples, the ceremonial travel of a Spanish royal governor was now of itself worthy of formal commemoration in print.

86. Ferrando Persia, *Relatione dei ricevimenti fatti in Mantova alla Maesta della Reina di Spagna dal Sereniss. Sig. Duca l'anno M.D.XCVIII del mese di novembre* (Mantua: Francesco Osanna, n.d.), 1 [BNP]. The account covers the reception at Revere as well as that in Mantua itself after the visit to Ferrara.

87. Mucantius, who had heavy managerial and ceremonial responsibilities during the queen's visit, devotes pp. 636–96 of his Latin diary to her entry and stay. See also Guarini, *Diario* II, fols. 47^r–53^v; and Minerbi, *Memorie*, fols. 102^r–109^v.

88. These accounts appear in a general list of expenses for the pope's journey, "Conti della Depositaria del Viaggio di Ferrara." They were published by J. A. F. Orbaan in a note of "Un viaggio di Clemente VIII nel Viterbese," *Archivio della R. Società Romana di Storia Patria* 36 (1913): 118–21. Other artists mentioned besides Guerra and Cesari are the sculptor Francesco Casella and Paolo Monferrato, both included in the Thieme-Becker *Künstler Lexikon*, and Ludovico Lanzi, not listed there. The prominent local artist Scarsellino is not mentioned in connection with the royal visit, although one notes he had been paid in August for work on a chasuble ordered by the pope.

89. See Mario Tutio, *Ordine et modo tenuto nell'incoronazione della Serenissima Moresina Grimaldi Dogaressa di Venetia. . . .* (Venice: Nicolò Peri, 1597) [BLL].

90. See Michelangelo Buonarroti il Giovane, *Descrizione delle felicissime nozze della Cristianissima Maestà di Madama Maria Medici Regina di Francia e di Navarra* (Florence: Marescotti, 1600) [BNCF].

91. The *Enciclopedia dello spettacolo* provides a good short survey of its development in the article "Gesuiti, teatro dei," whose Italian section was done by Giuseppe Pastina.

92. Rule 13 of the Rector, translation taken from Edward A. Fitzpatrick, *St. Ignatius and the "Ratio Studiorum"* (New York and London: McGraw-Hill, 1933), 140. The original Latin reads:

Tragoediarum et Comediarum, quas non nisi latinas et rarissimas esse oportet, argumentum sacrum si ac pium: neque quidquam actibus interponatur quod non latinum sit ac decorum: persona ulla muliebris vel habitus introducatur.

93. In the 1545 preface to his German translation of the apocryphal Book of Judith, Luther speculates that the ancient Hebrews may have set the story into drama as an example to their youth. *D. Martin Luthers Werke . . . Die Deutsche Bibel*, 12. Band (Weimar: Hermann Böhlaus Nachfolger, 1961), s. 7. In his preface to the apocryphal Book of Tobit (p. 109 of the same volume), he declares that Judith makes a fine subject for tragedy.

94. See Allan P. Farrell, *The Jesuit Code of Education: Development and Scope of the "Ratio Studiorum"* (Milwaukee: Bruce Publishing Co., 1938), 224–25 and 284.

95. Benedetto Soldati published the text from a manuscript in *Il collegio mamertino e le origini del teatro gesuitico* (Turin: Ermanno Loescher, 1908), 121–70.

96. The performance is famous in theater history. The best account is given in Grillo's *Breve trattato*, cited above, 31–56.

97. For the departure from Ferrara, see Mucantius's *Diarium*, 698–703; and Guarino's *Diario* II, fols. 54^r–56^v. The latter account is incomplete because leaf 57 is missing from the manuscript volume.

98. See the anonymous *Descrittione de gli apparati fatti in Bologna per venuta di N. S. Papa Clemente VIII. con gli disegni de gli archi, statue & pitture* (Bologna: Vittorio Benacci, 1598) [BNCF, Moren.].

99. For this entry too a *livret* was published: Odoardo Magliano, *L'ordine tenuto nel ricevere il Santissimo Sacramento nell'entrare in Roma. Con la processione, & apparati delle strade, da S. Maria del Popolo, à S. Pietro in Vaticano. Et l'entrata di nostro signore Papa Clemente Ottavo* (Rome: Bartholomeo Bonfadino, 1598) [Ariostea, Ang.]. For the trip back to Rome, and the entry, see as well Rocca, *De Sacrosancto Christi Corpore*, 103–115; and Mucantius's MS *Diarium*, 703–849.

100. *Annali* IV, fols. 273^r–278^r.

101. There were several efforts in the late quattrocento and early cinquecento to recreate the triumphal chariot, actually a more authentic classical revival than the temporary triumphal arch, but the form was abandoned in the later Renaissance. Louis XII must have discouraged the revivers when he refused to mount into a chariot prepared for him at Milan in 1509.

102. The best accounts of the two entries are found in the diary of the papal master of ceremonies Paride de' Grassi, *Il diario di Leone X . . .*, eds. Pio Delicati and Mariano Armellini (Rome: Tip. della Pace, 1884), 84–96 and 168–76 respectively for Bologna and Rome. Grassi had objected to the promiscuity of pagan and Christian themes that resulted from holding the Roman entry on Palm Sunday, but the pontiff had overruled him. See also, particularly for the texts of inscriptions, diplomatic reports sent to Venice and published in *I diarii di Marino Sanuto* (MCCCCXCVI–MDXXXIII), ed. Rinaldo Fulin et al. (Venice: F. Visentini, 1879–1913), vol. 6, cols. 491–93; and vol. 7, cols. 63–65, for the two entries.

103. See G. B. Borino's essay "Il contrastato trionfo," in the collectively authored volume *Il trionfo di Marc'antonio Colonna* (Rome: Società Romana di Storia Patria, 1938), 1–63.

104. The real Trajan's Column in Rome still has at its top Tommaso Della Porta's statue of Saint Peter with which Sixtus V had that of Trajan replaced in 1587.

The implication of a parallel between Peter and a pagan emperor was less shocking than a parallel with a reigning pope would have been.

105. The Archivio di Stato in Ferrara preserves some of the plans and suggestions in folder 45 of Libretto 30, Serie Patriarcale of the Archivio del Comune.

106. For a summary of the very complicated history of *divagazioni* of the Po since ancient times, and a résumé of hydraulic projects undertaken to control it, see Giacomo Savioli and Giacomo Menegatti's introduction to "Documenti sulla regolamentazione delle acque nel territorio ferrarese dal '600 al '800," in the *Quaderni di Ricerca*, no. 4 (1982), of the Archivio Storico, under the Assessorato alle Istituzioni Culturali, Comune di Ferrara.

107. See the *livret* by Rémy du Puys, *La tryumphante et solemnelle entree faicte sur le nouvel et joyeux advenement de treshault trespuissant et tresexcellent prince Monsieur Charles....* ([Paris]: Gilles de Gourmont, [1515]), edited in this series with an introduction by Sydney Anglo (Amsterdam: Theatrum Orbis; and New York: Johnson Reprint Corporation, n.d.). There was to be a new parallel to Ferrara's message in some festival *apparati* of 1635, when the cardinal-infante Ferdinand made a grand entry into Antwerp. That city had supplanted Bruges as the commercial center of Flanders, but now its own prosperity was declining, largely because of a blockade. The artist Peter Paul Rubens was engaged to portray the city's plight graphically to the entering prince. See Elizabeth McGrath, "Le Déclin d'Anvers et les décorations de Rubens pour l'entrée du Prince Ferdinand en 1635," in Jean Jacquot, ed., *Les Fêtes de la Renaissance* III (Paris: Centre National de la Recherche Scientifique, 1975), 173–86.

108. See p. 30 of Anglo's introduction to Du Puy's *livret*.

109. His account in the *Annali*, the best surviving, was published by Patrizio Antolini as *La solenne entrata in Ferrara di Lucrezia Medici venuta sposa al Duca Alfonso d'Este*, Nozze Carnevali-Saletti (Argenta: Tipografia Argentana, 1874). All of the following information concerning Rodi is taken or inferred from his *Annali*.

110. All of the following information about him is taken directly, or inferred, from the text of his book.

111. Bulgarelli's bibliography lists a number of such bulletins printed by him.

112. A good deal is known about his life and career. See Pio Paschini's biographical article "Rocca, Angelo" in the *Enciclopedia cattolica* (Vatican City: Ente per l'Enciclopedia Cattolica et il Libro Cattolico, 1953).

113. *Pontificis Maximi Clementis VIII. Anno MDXCVIII. Ferrariam Petentis & Ingredientis Apparatus & Pompa ... Auctore F. Angelo Rocca....* Excudebat Petrus Antonius MDCII. [Kansas, BLL]. A full bibliographical citation of this publication is given with the discussion of its provenance, in Appendix II.

114. Most of the following information about his life is taken from Jan Wladislaw Woś's introduction to the edition *Itinerario in Polonia del 1596 di Giovanni Paolo Mucante cerimoniere pontificio. Parte prima: Cracovia* (Rome: Il Centro di Ricerca, 1981).

115. See my *The Majesty of the State: Triumphal Progresses of Foreign Sovereigns in Renaissance Italy (1494–1600)*, (Florence: Olschki, 1986), 137–46.

116. *Relatione della reconciliatione, assolutione, et benedittione del Serenissimo Henrico Quarto ... fatta dalla Santità di N. S. Papa Clemente Ottavo ... con minuto ragguaglio di tutte le processioni, orationi, & cerimonie ... descritto da Gio. Pavolo Mucante....* (Viterbo: Appresso Agostino Colaldi, as Istanza di Ottaviano Gabrielli, 1595) [Vall., BNCF].

117. See Pastor, 24:112; and the *Itinerario*, cited in note 108 above.

118. There is an unimportant but curious mystery connected with a projected publication of excerpts from this work. In the eighteenth century the Canon Giovan Battista Gattico set out to prepare an anthology of accounts of papal travel as part of a work called *Acta Selecta Caerimonalia Sanctae Romanae ex Variis Mss. Codicibus et Diariis* (Romae: Apud Haeredes Jo. Laurentii Barbiellini, 1753). Mocante is included, but his narrative of the trip to Ferrara is broken off abruptly at the stage of Spoleto, and the whole anthology ends in mid-sentence on page 203. All five copies of the work I have seen are thus mutilated, and one of those in the Vatican Library bears a solemn handwritten notation: "Per ordine autorevole fu sospeso il proseguimento della presente opera, anzi ritirati furono li fogli già stampati." It is hard to imagine that anything subversive or dangerous was found in Mocante's chronicle.

119. A short history of diaries written by papal masters of ceremonies in the sixteenth century is given by L. Caetani in "Vita e diario di Paolo Alaleone maestro delle cerimonie pontificie 1582–1638," *Archivio della R. Società Romana di Storia Patria* 16 (1893): 5–39.

120. *Gli avvisi a stampa*, p. 17.

121. Quoted by Thomas Heywood in *Englands Elizabeth Her Life and Troubles* (London: Printed by I. Beale for P. Waterhouse, 1631), 229; and reproduced in David M. Bergeron, *English Civic Pageantry 1558–1642* (London: Edward Arnold, 1971), 18.

Bibliography

Contemporary Livrets *Dealing With the Pageantry in Ferrara*

For each event, the *livret* reproduced in this volume is listed first and has a somewhat fuller description. Thereafter the order is alphabetical. Many more *livrets* having to do with different, but related ceremonial events are described in the notes.

THE DEPARTURE OF CESARE D'ESTE
AND ENTRY OF THE CARDINAL-LEGATE

1. Anonymous. *Narratione della partenza del Sereniss. Sig. D. Cesare da Este duca di Modena & di Reggio & C. con le feste et trionfi fatte nell'intrata dell'Illustriss. et Reverendiss. Cardinale Aldobrandino legato.* Nella città di Ferrara, il dì 29 di Genaro. M.D.XCVIII. In Pavia, Appresso Andrea Viani, 1598. 4 unnumbered fols. Sig. A1-4. 19.5 x 14 cm. British Library shelfmark 811. d. 54 (4).

2. Anonymous. *Relatione della solenne intrata fatta nella città di Ferrara, il dì 29. di gennaro, 1598 dall'Illmo. et Rev^{mo}. S^r. Cardinal Aldobrandino Legato.* In Roma, Appresso li Stampatori Camerali, 1598. 2 unnumbered fols. [Vat., Lucca]

ENTRY OF CLEMENT VIII INTO FERRARA

3. Anonymous [Filippo Rodi?]. *Felicissima entrata di N.S PP. Clemente VIII. nell'inclita città di Ferrara. Con gli apparati publici fatti nelle città, terre, castelli, e luoghi, dove S. Santità è passata, dopò la sua partita di Roma.* Stampata in Ferrara, Per Vittorio Baldini, Stampator Camerale. Con licenza de i Superiori. 1598. 4 unnumbered fols. Sig. A1-4. 20 x 14 cm. British Library shelfmark 811 g. 30. [Other copies, with various places of publication but identical texts, in Ariostea, Vat., Arch., Moreniana-Riccardiana]

4. Anonymous. *Lettera venuta da Ferrara, la quale raguaglia la solenissi-*
   ma entrata della Santità di N. S. Clemente Papa VIII. in detta città,
   li 9 di maggio, 1598. Con l'intervento dell'Illustrissimi & Reverendiss.
   Cardinali, Ambasciatori de prencipi, & republiche. Et altri Reverendiss.
   Sig. prelati. Con infinito numero di nobiltà adornatissima. Romae, Apud
   Impressores Camerales, 1598. 2 unnumbered fols. [BLL, Vat.]

5. Banordini, Annibale. *Narratione dell'entrata pontificale fatta da la San-*
   tità di N. Sig. Clemente Papa VIII. Nella città di Ferrara, & di tutto
   l'ordine che si è tenuto in detta entrata. Raccolta da Annibale Banordini
   da Città di Castello. In Roma, Presso Bartholomeo Bonfadino, 1598.
   4 unnumbered fols. [Private collection of Mr. Mario Lanfranchi,
   Parma]

6. Rocca, Angelo. *De Sacro Sancto Christi Corpore, Romanis Pontificibus*
   Iter Conficientibus Praeferendo Commentarius. Antiquissimi Ritus Cau-
   sam et Originem, Variasque Summorum Pontificum Sacratissimi Sacramenti
   Clemente VIII. Pont. Max. Ferrariam Profisciente, Ejusdem Pontificis
   Solemnem in eam Civitatem Ingressum, et in Urbem Romam Reditum
   Complectens. Auctore F. Angelo Rocca Camerte Augustiniani Apostolici
   Palatii Sacrista. Romae, Apud Guillelmum Facciottum, 1599. Pp.
   72–92. [Columbia, BLL]

ENTRIES OF THE VENETIAN AMBASSADORS AND DUKE OF MANTUA

7. Amarotti, Gieronimo. *Narratione della solenissima entrata in Ferrara*
   del Serenissimo Duca di Mantoa. Et dell'Illustrissimi Ambasciatori di Vene-
   tia. Con il recivimento fattoli da N. Sig. Papa Clemente VIII. Raccolto
   da Gieronimo Amarotti. In Roma, Presso Bartholomeo Bonfadino,
   1598. 5 unnumbered fols. Sig. A1–5. Ca. 18.5 x 12 cm. British Library
   shelfmark: 9930. bb. 5. [Another copy, Ang.]

ENTRY OF THE DUKE OF PARMA

8. Greco, Vincenzo. *La reale entrata del Serenissimo Duca di Parma et*
   Piacenza &c. in Ferrara. Descritta da D. Vincenzo Greco, catanese. In
   Ferrara, Per Vittorio Baldini Stampatore Camerale, [1598]. 5 unnum-
   bered fols. Sigs. A1–5. 20 x 14 cm. Biblioteca Nazionale Centrale,
   Florence shelfmark: Misc. 1009. 25. [Other copies in Ariostea, Esten-
   se, Vall., BLL]

9. Ianni da Ischia, Antonio. *Viaggio fatto alla città di Ferrara dal Serenis-*
   simo Duca di Parma, Piacenza & Castro &c. Et la real'entrata di S.A.
   Seren^{ma}. con li nomi de' marchesi, conti, & cavallieri, numero de' paggi,

staffieri, & colori di livree, con il felicissimo suo ritorno alla città di Parma. Descritto da Antonio Ianni da Ischia. In Ferrara, & in Parma, 1598. 6 unnumbered fols. [Ariostea]

10. Muccante (Mocante), Gio. Paulo. *Relatione della solenissima intrata fatta in Ferrara. Dal Serenissimo Duca di Parma il dì 29. di giugno. 1598. Scritta da Gio. Paulo Muccante mastro de cerimonie.* In Roma, Appresso li Stampatori Camerali, 1598. 4 unnumbered fols. [Vall.]

THE ENTRY OF MARGARET AND ALBERT OF AUSTRIA
AND THE *SPOSALIZII*

11. Mocante, Gio. Paolo. *Relatione dell'entrata solenne fatta in Ferrara à di 13. di novembre 1598. Per la Sereniss. D. Margarita d'Austria Regina di Spagna: Et del Consistoro publico con tutti li preparamenti fatti dalla Santità di N. S. Clemente Papa VIII. per tal'effetto. Con minuto raguaglio della messa pontificale cantata da S. Beatitudine, & delle cerimonie delli sponsalitij fatti nella chiesa cathedrale di detta città, domenica alli 15. del medesimo, con la cerimonia della Rosa, che S. S. finita la messa donò alla Regina. Descritta da Gio. Paolo Mocante, uno de' maestri di cerimonie della cappella di S. Beatitudine. Ad istanza di Ottaviano Gabrielli.* In Roma, Appresso Nicolò Mutii, 1598. 8º. 12 unnumbered fols. Sigs. A1-4, B1-4, C1-4. 21 x 14 cm. British Library shelfmark: 9917. cc. 6. [Other copies in BNCF, Vall.]

12. Anonymous. *Entrata della Ser^ma Regina Margarita d'Austria, nostra sig., nell'inclita città di Ferrara, con gli sponsalitii di Sua Maesta, et della Sereniss. Infanta di Spagna. Scritta à un principalissimo Sig. di questa città.* Pavia, Andrea Viani, 1598. 8 numbered pages. [Pavia]

13. Anonymous. *La sontuosissima entrata della Serenissima Margherita d'Austria Regina di Spagna, & del Serenissimo Arciduca Alberto d'Austria in Ferrara. Dove s'intendono gli sponsalitii di questi due, così alti signori. Et l'allegrezze, fatti così da Sua Beatitudine in Ferrara, come dal Serenissimo di Mantova ne' suoi luochi, & ultimamente in Mantova.* In Verona, Per Francesco dalle Donne, & Scipione Vargnano suo genero, 1598. 4 unnumbered fols. [Ariostea]

14. Beccari, Bernardino. *Relatione della solenne entrata che hà fatto la Serenissima Reina di Spagna in Ferrara. A dì 13. di novembre 1598. Publicata per Bernardino Beccari alla Minerva.* In Roma, Per Nicolò Mutij, 1598. 4 unnumbered fols. [BLL, Vat.]

15. Beccari, Bernardino. *Relatione dello sposalitio della Serenissima D. Margherita d'Austria con il Cattolico Re Filippo III. Et della Serenissima In-*

*fanta D. Isabella di Spagna col Sermo. Arciduca Alberto seguiti nella cit-
tà di Ferrara a dì 15. d'ottobre 1598. Et di tutto quello che è seguito in-
detta città dall'arrivo di Sua Maestà fino alla sua partenza, che fu alli
18. del medesimo. Publicata per Bernardino Beccari alla Minerva.* 4 unnumbered fols. [Ang.] [A different edition with no author's name:
In Milano, Per Pandolfo Malatesta, Impressore Regio Camerale, BNP]

16. Grillo, Gio. Battista. *Breve trattato di quanto successe alla Maestà della
Regina D. Margherita N. S. dalla città di Trento fine d'Alemagna, e principio d'Italia fino alla città di Genova. Si dell'intrate superbe che fece
per ogni luogo che passò, come delle feste, archi trionfali, e presenti che
gli furno fatti da molti principi, & di ogn'altra cosa, che gli occorse. Raccolto per il Dottor Gio. Battista Grillo napolitano. Con le particolarita
del sponsalitio fatto nella città di Ferrara per mano della Santità di Papa
Clemente Ottavo* (In Napoli, Appresso Costantino Vitale, 1604),
19–30. [BNP, BLL, Genoa]

17. Reale, il Cavalier. *La felicissima entrata della Serenissima Regina di
Spagna, Donna Margarita d'Austria nella città di Ferrara il dì 13. novembre
MDXCVIII. Havuta dal Cavalier Reale.* In Ferrara, Per Vittorio Baldini [1598]. 4 unnumbered fols. [BLL, BNCF, Lucca; facsimile reprint
in Arch.]

18. Rocca, Angelo. *De Sacro Sancto Christi Corpore* . . . (see no. 6 above),
97–100.

19. Zerlii, Biagio. *Narratione del viaggio della Serenissima Margherita d'Austria Regina di Spagna. Cominciando da Ferrara, Ostiglia, Mantova, Cremona, & Lodi, per fino a Milano. Dove s'intende il sponsalitio di S. M.
. . . Raccolto da Biagio Zerlii veronese* (In Cremona, Appresso Barucino De Giovanni, 1599), fols. A2^r–A2^v. [BNP]

The Engravings

20. Tempesta, Antonio. *Vero disegno dell'ordine tenuto da Clemente VIII.
nel fel. ingresso di S. S^{tà}. nella città di Ferrara, l'anno 1598, cum privili-
gio summi pontificis, Antonio Tempesta in. et sculp.* Romae, 1598. Joseph
De Rubeis Junior Formis. [Dept. of Prints and Drawings, British
Museum]

21. Callot, Jacques, and Sciaminossi, Raffaello. Engravings 17, 18, and
19 from the *livret* of funeral services for Margaret of Austria, Queen
of Spain, held in Florence in 1612: Giovanni Altoviti, *Essequie della*

Sacra, Cattolica e Real Maestà di Margherita d'Austria celebrate dal Serenissimo Don Cosimo II gran duca di Toscana descritte da Giovanni Altoviti (In Firenze, Nella Stamperia di Bartolommeo Sermartelli e Fratelli, 1612). [Moren.] The series of twenty-five engravings purport to evoke high moments in the life of the dead queen. Of these, nine show scenes from her triumphal crossing of Italy in 1598–99.

Manuscript Diaries Containing
First-Hand Accounts of Some or All
of the Festive Events in Ferrara

22. Guarini, Marc'Antonio. *Diario tutte di le cose accadute nella nobilissima città di Ferrara principiando per tutto l'anno M.D.L.XX sino a questo dì et anno M.D.L.XXXVIII.* . . . 1 vol. Biblioteca Estense, Modena: MS. α. H. 2. 16.

23. Guarini, Marc'Antonio. *Diario . . . di tutte le cose al suo tempo accadute nella nobilissima citta di Ferrara principiando per tutto il dì. 28 di gennaio dell'anno presente 1598.* . . . 1 vol. Biblioteca Estense, Modena: MS. α. H. 2. 17.

24. Minerbi, Elia. *Memorie di Ferrara dal anno 1412 fino al anno 1607.* . . . 1 vol. Biblioteca Ariostea, Ferrara: MS. Classe 1ª, 759.

25. Mucantius, Joannes Paulus (Mocante or Muccante, Giovan Paolo). *De Itinere Clementis VIII. Pontificis Opt. Max. Ferrariam versus Rebusque Gestis in eadem Civitate et de eius Reditu ad Urbem et Reliquiis quae Acciderunt per totum Annum M.D.II.C.* Archivio di Stato, Modena: MS. Cancelleria Ducale; Documenti di Stato e Citta, busta 122. This account, 907 pages in length, constitutes the fourth volume of Mucantius's papal diary. Other copies of the diary in the Vatican and Corsiniana Libraries, Rome.

26. Rodi (or Roddi), Filippo. *Annali di Ferrara, Libri V.* 4 bound vols. Biblioteca Estense, Modena: MS. α. H. 3. 7–10. Another copy, less legible, in the Ariostea, Ferrara.

Manuscript Records of Expenditures by the Comune For Street Apparati in the Triumphal Entries

28. Archivio di Stato, Ferrara: Archivio del Comune, Serie Patrimoniale, Lib. 30, nos. 17 and 53, dealing with preparations for the entries of the cardinal and the pope, respectively. (Analogous records for the queen's entry have not survived.)

Appendix I

Principal Ferrarese Entries
From the Death of Borso d'Este in 1471
to the Devolution in 1598

1. 1473, July 3 — Grand entry of Eleonora d'Aragona, daughter of King Alfonso I of Naples and bride of Duke Ercole I. The anon. *Diario ferrarese*, ed. Giuseppe Pardi, *RIS*, parte 7, vol. 1, pp. 88–89.
2. 1502, February 2 — Entry of Lucrezia Borgia, daughter of Pope Alexander VI and bride of the future duke Alfonso I. Bernardino Zambotti, *Diario ferrarese dall'anno 1476 sino al 1504*, ed. Giuseppe Pardi, *RIS*, tomo 24, parte 7, vol 2, pp. 312–15.
3. 1528, December 1 — Entry of Renée de France, daughter of the late king Louis XII and bride of the future duke Ercole II. Gasparo Sardi, *Libro delle historie ferraresi.* . . . (Ferrara: Gius. Gironi, 1646), 7–8.
4. 1543, April 21 — Entry of Pope Paul III, returning to Rome after visiting the newly acquired papal cities of Parma and Piacenza. An anonymous *Lettera nuova de tutte le entrate feste giostre comedie e doni per la venuta di P. P. III. a Ferrara cosa molto bella* (N.p, n.d.; but probably Ferrara, 1543) [BLL, Arsenal]; and an anonymous *Trionfo dato alla Santità di Nostro Signore Papa Paulo Terzo nella inclita città di Ferrara* (N.p., n.d.; but probably Ferrara or Rome, 1543) [Ariostea].
5. 1559 — Entry and official reception of Alfonso II d'Este, returning home to assume the dukedom after the death of his father. An anonymous *La creatione del Sig. Donno Alfonso II duca quinto di Ferrara* (N.p., n.d.; but probably Ferrara, 1559) [Arch.].
6. 1560, February 19 — Entry of Lucrezia de' Medici, daughter of Duke Cosimo I of Florence and bride of Duke Alfonso II of Ferrara. See the contemporary account of Filippo Rodi, published by P. Antolini as *La solenne entrata in Ferrara di Lucrezia Medici venuta sposa al Duca Alfonso d'Este*, Nozze Carnevali-Saletti, (Argenta: Tipografia Argentana, 1894).

7. 1565, December 1–Entry of Barbara d'Austria, daughter of the emperor Ferdinand I and second bride of Duke Alfonso II. See the anonymous *Narratione particular del'intrata della Sereniss. Principessa Barbara d'Austria in Ferrara & delle feste e trionfi fatti nelle nozza celeb. con l'Illust. et Ecc. S. Duca di Fer. suo consorte* (N.p.,n.d.; but probably Ferrara, 1565) [BNP].

8. 1569, May 7–Entry of the archduke Charles of Austria, brother of Duchess Barbara d'Austria. See Ludovico Antonio Muratori, *Delle antichità estensi . . . parte II* (Modena: Nella Stamperia Ducale, 1740), 396.

9. 1574, July 28–Entry of King Henry III of France (Henry IV of Poland), on his way home from Cracow to assume the crown of France. See an account by the Ferrarese *letterato* Pirro Ligorio, published by Pierre de Nolhac and Angelo Solerti in *Il viaggio in Italia di Enrico III re di Francia e le feste a Venezia, Ferrara, Mantova, e Torino* (Turin: L. Roux, 1890), 321–33.

10. 1579, February 25–Entry of Margherita Gonzaga, daughter of Duke Guglielmo of Mantua and third bride of Duke Alfonso II. See a detailed account from the MS diary of M. A. Guarini, published in Angelo Solerti, *Ferrara e la corte estense nella seconda metà del secolo decimosesto. I discorsi di Annibale Romei gentiluomo ferrarese* (Città di Castello: S. Lapi, 1891), xxx–xxxvii.

Appendix II

Concerning the Unauthorized 1602 Re-edition of Passages from Angelo Rocca's De Sacrosancto Corpore, 1599

Pontificis Maximi Clementis VIII. Anno MDXCVIII. Ferrariam Petentis & Ingredientis Apparatus & Pompa. Expressa cum Fide ex Libro Romae Edito Anno 1599. apud Guillelmum Facciottum, sub Titolo; De Sacrosancto Corpore Romanis Pontificibus Praeferendo Commentarius &c. Auctore F. Angelo Rocca Camerte Augustiniano, Apostolici Palatii Sacrista. Et Pagina Edita Primum Romae, Deinde Venetiis Italicè, per Girolanum Portum 1598. Excudebat Petrus Antonius Anno M D CII. 30 numbered pages. [Kansas, BLL, BNP]

The re-edition is clearly an unauthorized one put out by an editor and a publisher with anti-papal opinions. The accounts of the journey of the *Corpus Domini* and of Clement's entry are taken faithfully from Rocca's treatise of 1599, but they are preceded by a short consolation to Christian princes who have had their rightful possessions taken away by Roman pontiffs (3–14), and followed (29–30) by *exempla* of great princes of the past who are recorded as having made *modest* entries into conquered cities. The consolatory essay has a pointed reference to Christ's injunction to "render unto Caesar that which is Caesar's," long a favorite text of those opposed to the temporal power of the popes. The exemplary rulers cited include the Eastern Roman Emperor Heraclius, who humbly returned the true cross to Jerusalem in A.D. 631 after some victories over the heathen Persians; and the eleventh-century crusader Godefroy de Bouillon, who rejected a crown offered him at the gate of the same city.

It is natural to think first of the possibility of a Protestant printer, and the British Library cataloguer suggests Geneva as the place of publication. That speculation is bolstered by the fact that the little work is bound together with some anti-papal passages from the *History of Italy* of the Florentine statesman and political theorist Francesco Guicciardini, who had died more than half a century before.[1] These passages, which include an analysis of the origin and growth of the temporal power of the popes, had been left out of editions of Guicciardini done in Italy, but had already been printed in Geneva in 1569.[2] There are, however, in the re-edition of Rocca, no evocations of doctrinal questions, and purely political motivations for the publication seem as likely as religious ones.

No other Catholic state of the period showed so much tolerance to critics of papal policy as did Venice, and that republic was moving toward the open conflict with Rome that would culminate in open defiance of a papal interdict in 1606–1607. Moreover, Venice is mentioned on the title page as one place of publication for a supposed original Italian version of the commentary. The earlier publisher is identified as "Girolanus Portus," very near indeed to the name of an actual Venetian publisher of the time, Girolamo Porto. As a further piece of evidence, one may note that "Petrus Antonius," mentioned as having brought out the 1602 book, was a pen name to be used later during the great confrontation with Rome by Pietro Antonio Ribetti, the Vicar General of Venice, in a treatise supporting the republic's stand published by himself, Paolo Sarpi, and five other theologians.[3] The Republic of Saint Mark may well have allowed, even sponsored, the curious 1602 edition of Rocca's pageantry account. Or perhaps Protestants in Geneva or Basel took a work that was being circulated in manuscript form by the Venetians and put it into print.

Notes to Appendix II

1. *Francisci Guicciardini . . . Loci Duo . . . Qui ex Ipsius Historiarum Libris III et IIII . . . Detracti, in Exemplaribus Hactenus Impressis non Leguntur, Nunc . . . Latinè, Italicè, Gallicèque Editi. . . .* Excudebat Petrus Antonius, 1602. The type and format of this publication are identical to those of the Rocca re-edition, and it seems clear that they are from the same printer.

2. *Francisci Guicciardini . . . Loci Duo, ob Rerum Quas Continent Gravitatem Cognitioni Dignissimi . . . Qui ex Ipsius Historiarum Libris III et IIII, Dolo Malo Detracti in Exemplaribus Hactenus Impressi Non Leguntur. . . .* (Basileae, 1569) [BNP].

3. *Trattato dell'interdetto della Santità di Papa Paulo V. nel quale si dimostra, che egli non è legitimamente publicato . . . composto dalli sottoscritti theologi, Pietro Antonio Archidiacono, F. Paulo de' Servi. . . .* (Venice, 1606) [BLL]. In a Latin edition of this treatise brought out in 1610, Ribetti is referred to as "Petrus Antonius."

Facsimiles

Bibliographical Note

I. The Departure of Cesare d'Este and Entry of the Cardinal-Legate reproduced from the British Library copy 811.d.54. Actual size.

II. The Entry of Pope Clement reproduced from the British Library copy 811 g. 30. Actual size.

III. The Entries of the Venetian Ambassadors and of the Duke of Mantua reproduced from the British Library copy 9930.bb.5. Actual size.

IV. The Entry of the Duke of Parma reproduced from the Firenze, Biblioteca Nazionale copy 218. Slightly reduced.

V. The Entry and *Sposalizio* of Margaret of Austria reproduced from the British Library copy 9917.CC.6. Actual size.

NARRATIONE
DELLA PARTENZA

DEL SERENISS. SIG. D. CESARE DA ESTE,
Duca di Modena, & di Reggio, & c.

CON LE FESTE ET TRIONFI

FATTE NELL'INTRATA DELL'ILLVSTRISS. ET
Reuerendiss. Cardinale Aldobrandino Legato.

Nella Città di Ferrara, il dì 29. di Genaro, M. D. XCVIII.

In Pauia, Appresso Andrea Viani, 1598.

Lamento fatto nella Partenza del Sereniss. D. Cesare, Duca di Modena, & Reggio, &c. Insieme con le feste, e Trionfi fatti nell'Intrata del l'Illustriss. & Reuerendiss. Card. Aldobrandino.

MERCORDI a 15. hore, che fu li 28. Genaro si partì il Duca da questa Città con questo ordine: dal Giardino del Castello fin'alla porta de gl'Angeli, che è vna strada diritta, larga, & longa quasi vn miglio, faceuano ala da circa 500. tra soldati pedoni, & caualli armati, questi al l'ariuar d'alcuni nobili à cauallo, cominciarono à marchiare dietro il lor Capitano, cadendo una sottile, & lenta pioggia, che faceua il giorno più infausto di quel che era. veniua la Duchessa con la figliuola dentro vna lettica ammalata, & malenconica, che haueua quasi dispersa la notte auanti, & dietro in vn'altra lettica veniuano li figliuolini. poi in tre carozze à sei caualli veniuano le sue damigelle, & suoi gentil'huomini particolari. Seguiua pur in carozza il Duca con quattro gentil'huomini, & ben fu di macigno, e di diamante chi tenne l'occhio asciutto a quel funebre, & compassioneuole spettacolo: non si sentiua altro romore, che quel delle carozze; perche le trombe delle Cornette, & di tamburi, di pedoni, & le lingue de' circonstanti erano muti, e mesti, considerando ogn'vno, come Deposuit potentes de sede, & exaltauit humiles. Perche se la Città non se gli rendeua, & se Fior. & Mant. non gli hauessero insidiato questo à sorprenderli Bersello, & quella la Graffignana, il Duca non si rendeua, & questa guerra haurebbe imitata quella di Troia, che durò dieci anni, e Dio sa poi, se al fin fosse poi stata presa, che tal relatione diedero il Sig. Mario Farnese, che lauorò à questi forti vestito da Contadino, & vn'altro gentilhuomo pur vestito da villano, che passò per la Romagna, & hoggidi si trastolano questi Capitani, & alfieri à considerar come si sia resa vna sì forte Città senza pur sfodrar spada; ma lasciamo questo, & notisi che quanto hò scritto, ò sono per scriuer, hollo veduto, hollo sentito io, & non per relatione, ma con gli, & con l'orecchie mie proprie. Vn'hora auanti la partita del Duca, furono liberati tutti li prigionieri del Palazzo, etiam quelli, che vi interueniua l'interesse del terzo, & quelli del Castello erano stati liberati qualche giorno inanzi per gratia speciale fatta hora à questo, hora à quell'altro gentilhuomo, che gli'el domandaua, da vn in poi, chiamato Alodminco, che fu mandato prigione à Modena; & tanto basta di questo per buon rispetto.

L'istesso giorno à 21. hore, furono publicati li Capitoli (quelli però che volsero manifestar essi) Ch'è s'erano accordati tra N. S. & il Duca tra quelli (perche furono quindeci) si conteneua questo. Che N. S. Benedicesa il Duca, & suoi seguaci ampliamente; Che tutte le possessioni, fabriche, Osterie, Passi, & simil beni, gioie, oro, & simili fossero del Duca, insieme con la metà dell'Artiglieria, & potesse condur essi suoi beni onunque gli piacesse, onero la rendita d'essi à suo beneplacito; Il medesimo à quelli, che lo seguiuano, che non fossero questi suoi seguaci per alcun tempo stretti à rihabitar quì, anzi possino annualmente condur via le lor Intrate. Che lui non possa intrar in Ferrara con gente armata; che volendo la Chiesa comprar qualunque

de'

A 2

de' ſuoi beni.ſia tenuto darglieli à giuſto prezzo ; Che il Caſtello habbia per confine quanto circonda la Foßa,ma le fabriche fuori di detta Foßa ſieno del Duca . Che Carpi ſia reſa adorna di Veſcouado . Che li renontia Ferrara,& ſue pertinentie . Che N.S.gli obliga 15. milla ſacchi di Sale ogn'anno da condurre a Ceruia ſu per il Pò fin alli Stati del Duca. Che reſti al Duca titoli,& honori di preſidenza,che haueua il Duca Alfonſo di fel.mem . Coſi a ſuon di trombe fu intimato al popolo per publico Araldo al ſolito .

GIOVEDI , che fu li 29. Genaro à 21.hore, arriuò l'antiguardia dell'Illuſtriſs.Cardmale Aldobrandino,cioè 26.Inſegne di pedoni tra archibugieri,& piche di 160. in 200. ſoldati l'una,& otto Cornette di cauallaria tra lanze , & archibugieri,& la retroguardia che entrò fuor di notte fu di 14. Inſegne di pedoni , & dieci Cornette . Veniua alla sfilata carriaggi,ſomari,& muli in gran quantità tra quali 46. muli del Cardinale belliſſimi,con bel ordine,à quali ſeguiuano 200. caualli di Gentilhuomini,che l'accompagnauano non chiamati da lui ; ma poi vi erano 95.nobili tra Romani,& Romagnuoli,che l'accompagnauano riccamente guarniti.

· Seguiuano li Religioſi Clauſtrali,con le lor Croci,& Candelabri di argento ; poi le Arti della Città con lor Confaloni auanti, poi il Clero in nobil , & bel ordine, con la Mula del Veſcouo menata à mano,riccamente guarnita . perche Sua Sig.Reueren diſs.era a piedi alla porta della Città il Veſcouo,che aſpettaua il Cardinale,che toſto gionſe, doue comparue ſotto eſſa porta (che di Caſtel Tealto ſi chiama) il Giudice de' 12. Saui con eſſi Saui,& qui con ſommiſſione il Giudice, cioè Tribuno della plebe , preſentò al Sig. Cardinale tre bacili,due d'argento, che vi erano ſopra le Chiaui della Città, e l'altro bacile indorato haueua ſopra vna Ceſtelleita coperta con le Chiaui del Caſtel dentro,che ſono d'argento indorate, & il Cardinale li poſe le mani ſopra chinandoſi, e ridendo con maeſtà , & affabilità inſieme, conſegnando quei bacili a tre palafrenieri,che ſe li poſero in capo , & s'inuiorno auanti il Cardinale a caminar in ordinanza con gli altri . Entrati dentro , comparuero 22. giouenetoi Cittadini , con vn Baldachin di broccato bianco,& coperto il Cardinale, che caualcaua in Pontificale ſopra la Mula , & entrati ſopra il primo Arco trionfale , furono ſentiti vari muſici inſtrumenti,& voci eßaltar le lodi ſue,come anco auenne nel paßar gli altri dui Archi fatti per honorarlo,andauano à dietro il Veſcouo di Ferrara, ch'era à pie di,riccamente guarniti ſoora ſuperbiſſimi Corſieri . Il Giudice de' 12. Saui , & eſſi Sauij . Il Sig.Loſano Conte,il Sig. Gio.Antonro Orſino, il Sig. Mario Farneſe, il Marcheſe Pepoli,il Marcheſe Aſcanio della Cornia,il Sig.Martio Colonna,il Duca Gaetano di Sermoneta,& dietro tutti,perche erano à due à dne,il Colonello Pietro Maluezi,queſti ſotto il Baldachino,veniua l'Illuſtriſs.Cardinale benedicendo continuamente da ambi i lati . dietro il Baldachino gli Arciueſconi Matteucci, & di Bologna,che queſto era gionto in Ferrara la ſera auanti,& alloggiato in Veſcouato, li Veſcoei di Reggio,Comacchio,Furlì,Ceſena,Faenza, & Bertinora. A queſta gran caualcata faceua ala la guardia di cento Labardiari tutti dello Stato di Meldola ve-la vestiti d'azurro, & giallo. Scaualcò in piazza alla porta del Domo, oue si pose la beretta, & su li scalini con le solite cerimonie tolse il possesso, tolse la perdonanza, e tornò fuori, & così à piedi andò al Castello ad alloggiar nel ricco appartamento dello specchio, che stà à parato di quel del Duca.

La prima Insegna di Fanti, che arriuò, andò al Castello imediate, doue piantò sul riuellino l'Insegna, e sopra la Torre, che risguarda la piazza vn Gonfalone. Gli Sbirri con il Barigello di Roma, che venne con la detta Insegna, menarono di fuori vn prigione, & con lui presero possesso nell'istesso tempo delle Carcere, & subito posero fuora la corda; l'altre insegne, secondo che arriuauano si distribuiuano vna per ogni porta della Città.

Furono nell'intrar S.S.Illustriss.& anco per tre notte seguenti, veduti; & sentiti vari fuochi, artiglieria, & raggi artificiati, & vociferatione della plebe, se ben non fu gettato danari.

Durò la detta caualcata dalle 21.hora fin'alla sera scura, & à due hore di notte andò à visitar la Sig.Duchessa d'Vrbino ammalata da catarro, & di febre, ma per vna via secreta, che lei ne tiene le Chiaui.

VENERDI, che fu li 30. Genaro, la Communità mādò à presentar à S.S.Illustris.l'infrascritte cose, cioè 18.Fachini carichi di Corbe di pesci di Mare eletto, & sei carichi di pesce dolce, come Sturioni, Trutte, Carpioni, & simili, così questi come quei di Mare pesci tutti grandissimi, & marauigliosi, pesce armato di piu sorte, quattro Cestoni portati da due fachini l'vno; due fachini carichi di speciaria intiera; due di zuccaro; due di Cere da tauola, & quattro di Torzi; due fachini carichi di Salami, e Salamoni stupendi; vna stangata di Fagiani numero 30.para, vna stangata di Pernici numero 60.para; vn'altra d'Indiani numero 18.para 10.Caprioli, otto vitelli, sei Daini, sei Cinghiari, & sei Ceruoni grandissimi; innanzi tutte le predette cose andauano inghirlandati due boui bianchi grandissimi impastati à panatella, & altre cosette, che non mi raccordo, lequali in tutto ascendono al valor di due mille scudi, e non mi vanteria, perche hò veduto, & stimato il tutto.

L'istesso giorno si trouò S.Sig.Illustriss.risentita di riscaldagione, ma non già portò altro danno, che di tosse, & sputo.

La notte auanti li soldati predetti, che erano 10. mille pedoni, & 2. mille caualli alloggiorno à discretione con tanta mala sodisfattione de' Cittadini, perche buttauano giu le porte, & voleuano tutto quello, che li facea bisogno per reficiarsi dal fango, & dalla fame, sete, e freddo, che danneggiorno ogn'uno sul viuo. è ben vero, che il Venerdì il Colonna lor Generale gridò à gl'Alfieri così suoi, come quelli della Città non hauessero assignato il suo Sestiero, & quelli si scusauano.

Il Sig.Pietro Maluezi co'l suo terzo se n'andò à casa sua, & molti altri Capitani, & Alfieri tornarono in Romagna, il Venerdì, & il Sabbato restando solo i Presidi alle porte, & alcuni pochi caualli.

L'istesso giorno à suon di trombe prohibì gl'archibuggi, concedendo l'armi con la
Lume,

Lume, sotto pene di corda, & il medesimo à chi molestasse gli Hebrei, fin che se ne fa ceua altra prouisione.

SABBATO à 21. hora andò per la Città in carozza con la solita sua guardia, senza hauer con lui niun Ferrarese, benedicendo ogn'vno, & scoprendosi il capo d'alcuni con molta affabilità, & maniera attrattina, e non v'era altra carozza, che la sua.

DOMENICA mattina comparse alla Messa in Domo, done dal Giudice, & 12. Saui, & sei della gionta fu giurato, & prestato il solito maggio, gridandosi vi ua Papa Clemente, & la Chiesa, & allhora di fu la porta del Domo il Tesoriero gettò al popolo 300. scudi tutte piastre d'argento da vna da 40. l'vna.

Partì quella mattina il Vescouo di Bertinora à pigliar il possesso di Romagna; & l'istessa mattina restò à disinare S. Sig. Illustrissima con tutti quei Prelati, Principi, & Signori, seruiti da gli scalchi, & ministri del Duca Alfonso bo. mem. & certo fu bellissima, & ricchissimo il desinare in principio, mezo, & fine.

Dopò desinare, perche pione, s'attese à spedir certi Dottori giouени Cittadini per Podestà di molte ville di questo Territorio, ma non si sà per quanto tempo, ilche hà dato sodisfattione grandissima à questi Cittadini, vedendo distribuir gli Vfficij tra loro.

LVNEDI mattina pur in Domo alla Messa maggiore detta medesimamente dal Vescouo di Ferrara, dispensò le Candelle al Clero, & à tutta la nobiltà un gran numero, & fece gettar via circa 50. scudi.

L'istesso giorno comparnero li 22. giouenetti, che li portarono i Baldachino, tutti vestiti di broccato biauco, & S. Sig. Illustrissima, hauendoli fatto donar 500. scudi, oltra al Baldachino, gli fece tutti Cauallieri, cingendoli lo Stocco, & calzandoli vno sperone à tutti, & donando così à ciascuno di loro, come anco à 38. gentildonne, che si trouarono presente, vna Medaglia d'oro, & vna d'argento per vno di valor quella d'oro scudi quattro, e questa d'argento d'vna Osella di coteste, con l'impronto sopra da vu lato la sua testa, & arma; dall'altra, Ferrara racquistata; & con vn breue Sermone s'esebi protettor loro.

Narratione come erano fatti gli Archi Trionfali nell'Intrata dell'Illustriss.
Cardinale Aldobrandino.

L'Arco primo era dedicato alla Gloria; Hauea nella sommità dell'vltimo fastigio vn Gonfalone della Chiesa, alla destra San Pietro, & alla sinistra San Paolo. Nel mezo vn'arma del Pontefice sostenuta dalla gloria, e dall'honore. Dall'altro gli erano la Concordia, & la Pace, che sostenevano due arme del Cardinale Aldobrandino. Nell'ordine sopra le colonne v'era due Statue, cioè la Giustitia, & la Diligentia appoggiate à due palme, con due tauole con le seguenti inscrittioni.

Cle-

Clemente viij. Pontifice Max.& gloriosiss. mensis magnitudinis intuitum diuinitaris,inuictæq; iustitiæ fortitudine victoriosissimi.

Petri Cardin. Eminentiss. qui mirificis proprie vigilantie Consilis victor angustissimo, pijssimo Concordi, & pacis amore superatus est.

Glorie immortali.

Il secondo arco era dedicato all'eternità alla sommità si era l'arma del Pontifice; da lati due arme del Cardinale sostenute da Fanciulli.

A man destra

V'era dipinto la Istoria in vno quadro in sembianza di scriuer. In vn altra vn ramo di Melagrano Simbolo della Concordia, e sra le colonne sopra vn pedistallo la Scoltura.   A man sinistra.

Pollinia vna delle Muse all'incótro della Istoria l'erba melissa,all'incontro del Melagrano,e fra le colonne la pittura,erani vna sol tauola con le seguenti inscrittioni.   Rerum ab illis preclarissime ac diuinitatus gestarum quas nulla delibit obliuio ab inuictissimis etiam frustra petitarum aut omnino intentatarum.

Æternæq; nominis, & æternitati.

Il terzo era dedicato alla Felicità .   Nel mezo v'era l'arma del Pontefice sostenuta dalla Clementia,& dalla Pace, con il Gonfalone di Roma sopra. Da lati la virtù, e l'honore,che sosteneuano l'armi del Cardinale , vi erano due quadri per due Storie. Sopra l'Arco era dipinto l'arco celeste, che scacciando le nuuole,serenaua il Cielo. Et erani vna tauola con l'infrascritta inscrittione,laquale riferendosi etiandio à gl'altri Archi, conteneua la dedicatione di tutti tre.

Felicitati quà, fuga sis teterrimi belli Nubis , & perpetua pacis serenitate reducta sanctiss. tanti Pontif. Clementia,& Clementiss. Card. virtus .

S.   P.   Q.   F.

Numini Maieflatiq; earum dedicatissimus.
Summa fide, & Religiose Conseruauit.

IL FINE.

FELICISSIMA
ENTRATA
di N.S PP. Clemente VIII.
nell'Inclita Città di Ferrara.

Con gli Apparati publici fatti nelle Città, Terre, Castelli, e Luoghi, doue S. Santità è passata, dopò la sua partita di Roma.

IN FERRARA, Per Vittorio Baldini, Stampator Camerale.
Con licenza de i Superiori. 1598.

Partita di Nostro Signore di Roma, per Ferrara.

Opo la partita del santissimo Sacramento, che fu di Domenica il Lunedì seguente à 13. d'Aprile nostro Signore, celebrò la Messa bassa, ne l'Altare maggiore de' santi Apostoli, con l'interuento de' Cardinali, & finita la Messa depose i parameti, e prese la Mozeta, e Stola, e s'inginocchiò nel Faldistorio auanti l'Altare, e con voce alta cominciò l'Antifona. In Viam pacis, &c. con li Versicoli & Orationi. Dipoi preso il perdono in S. Pietro se ne vscì per la porta di S. Maria della Febre verso campo Santo, & iui montò in Lettica, accompagnato dall'Illustrissimi Cardinali fino à porta Angelica, cioè

Dal Cardinal di Como.   Dal Cardinal Sauli.   Dal Cardinal Ascoli.
Dal Cardinal Mattei.   Dal Cardinal Aquauiua.   Dal Cardinal Pepoli.
Dal Cardinal Peretti.   E quando furono arriuati alla Porta, sua Santità fece voltare la Lettica, e diede la Benedittione alli sopradetti Cardinali, li quali tornorono à dietro, e sua Santità seguì il viaggio.

In prima cominciò la caualcata de cariaggi.
Le Lettiche, e le chinee menate à mano da Famigli di Stalla vestiti di rosso.
Le Valigie di sua Santità.
Vna squadra di caualli Leggieri, con quattro Trombette.
La Famiglia del Papa, cioè Camerieri Secreti, Trinciante, Medico, Coppiere.
Li Sguizzari à piedi, con li Archibugi & Alabarde.
Il Gouernatore di Roma, ilquale l'accompagnò passato ponte Molo.
Il Crucifero con la Croce. Nostro Signore, nella Lettica.
Dipoi seguiua gl'Illustrissimi Cardinali sopra le lor Mule, con l'ombrelle, ouero parasoli, che furno.
Il Cardinal Baronio.   Il Cardinal Arigon.
Il Cardinal del Monte.   Il Cardinal S. Giorgio.
Don Pietro Orsino Vescouo   Vescouo di Cauiglion.
Et à ponte Molo vi arriuò il Cardinal Bianchetto, il Cardinal Burghese, & il Cardinal Cesis, con le sue carozze.
Il Tesauriere della Camera andò prima auanti.
Altri Prelati lo seguirono doppo, chi à cauallo, & chi in carozze.
La prima sera alloggiò à Castel nuouo con gran confusione, per la picciolezza del luogo, & per la moltitudine grande di caualli, e gente.
A Ciuità Castellana Martedì sera, pur con non poca confusione, abbrucciandosi vna stalla, vn fenile, due caualli, & molte selle; la mattina si passò il Teuere con vn ponte fatto artificiosamente di molte barche.
A Narni, Mercordì sera fu riceuuto nobilissimamente, & entrò per la porta Romana, essendo per tutto'l corso della strada, per donde doueua passare, eretti otto Archi trionfali bellissimi, due de' quali erano fuori della detta porta, tutti con epitaffi, motti, & versi assai graui, oltre tre fonti, due nelle piazze, l'altra fuori della

rì della porta delle Riuolte, superbamente adornati, & con versi volgari dottamente composti, sopra la memoria di Papa Giouanni, di Nerua Imperatore, & di Gattamelata, prodotti da questa Città, della quale s'io volessi descriuere il tutto, & il mirabile ordine tenuto in questa entrata, farei vergogna all'altre: ma chi desidera intendere il tutto minutamente legga la Narratione mandata dal Sig. Tito Agostini, al Sig. Caualier Regale Fusoricco da Narni, Trinciante dell'Illustrissimo, & Reuerendiss. Sig. Card. Montalto, che intenderà cose merauigliose.

A Terni, Giouedì sera fù riceuuto à Collescipoli con apparati, e fontane di vini, & Sua Santità andò a pranzo alla Cascata di piede luco, e la sera à Terni, & era fatta tenda per tutta la strada, e si stette commodamente, e fu incontrato da fanciulli vestiti di ormesino bianco, & riccamente addobbati.

A Spolti, Venerdì fù riceuuto da 24. giouani grandi vestiti di ormesino di rose secche, e riccamente addobbati, con le mazze in mano.

A Foligno, Sabbato sera, doue si vide gran moltitudine di popolo, fecero vn'arco con la statua di Sua Santità finta di bronzo, & altre statue, e fù incontrata da molti fanciulli vestiti con camise di cendale bianco, con vn ramo d'oliua in mano.

A Camerino, Domenica, vi erano più archi, & nella piazza fuochi artificiati, che abbrucciorno sino il Campanile e fù presentato a Sua Santità dall'Illustrissimo Sig. Cardinal Camerino grandissima copia di vettouaglie necessarie.

A Macerata, Lunedì sera fu riceuuto a pranso a Calderola dall'Illustrissimo Signor Cardinale di Cosenza, oue fece corte bandita copiosamente; la sera poi entrò di notte alquanto stracco, e si riposò tutto Mercordì.

A Loreto, Giouedì sera con molta stretta, e calca, & Venerdì Sua Beatitudine disse la Messa nella S. Casa, & communicò alcuni, oltre alli Camerieri secreti. Sabbato, & Domenica mattina fece il simile, e donò vna bellissima Croce con sei Candelieri d'argento, e due gambe medesimamente d'argento massiccie, e mille scudi nella cassa, & il paramento ricchissimo con il quale S. S. celebrò la S. Messa.

In Ancona, Domenica sera, doue si vidde vn bellissimo apparato, e molti archi, statue, & fu incontrato da 24. giouani vestiti di turchino, con molte gioie adornati, dapoi fu riceuuto nobilissimamente in Vescouato da Monsig. Conti, il quale li fece due sontuosissimi banchetti, & medesimamente a tutta la Corte, con bellissimo ordine, & in particolare tre tauole nel Cortile per collatione a' palafrenieri de' Cardinali, Sguizzeri, e Caualli leggieri, quali tauole erano, oltre alle cose mangiatiue piene, ma arricchite di pastizzi fatti a statue in diuerse maniere messe ad oro, con molte sorti di confettioni, & Sua Beatitudine pigliò molto gusto in vedere l'apparecchio, e poi l'assalto, che vi fu fatto. Lunedì sera poi furono fatti infiniti luminari, tiri, e girandole, & in particolare in Mare vi erano, oltre le tre galere Venetiane, e naui, vn'arco trionfale fabricato sopra due gran vascelli, al quale fu dato fuoco, & caminaua con grandissima moltitudine di razzi, e trombe di fuoco, che pareua ardesse l'acque. Martedì sera poi arriuo l'Illustriss Sig. Cardinale Aldobrandino, il quale fu incontrato da molti Cardinali, e si fece grande allegrezza. Mercordì poi Sua Santità disse la Messa piana nel Domo, qual'era pieno di popolo, e poi al Vespró: e doppò andorno molti Cardinali a spasso sù le galere, con il Generale di esse, qual'era il Clariss. Giustiniano, & N. S. lo fece Cavaliere, & li donò vna grossa catena d'oro, con vna medaglia del suo impronto.

Giovedì mattina giorno dell'Ascensione, si fece Capella nel Domo, doue Sua Beatitudine vdì la Messa con 15. Cardinali, e poi fù portata S. Sātità in vn palco ben apparato, cō il baldachino portato dal Magistrato, e diede la Benedittione; e tutte tre le fortezze sparorno grossissimi pezzi d' Artiglieria, dapoi si partì il santissimo Sacramento per Sinigaglia, doue fù riceuto sontuosissimamente da S. Alt.

Venerdì, che fu il primo giorno di Maggio, à hore 21 entrò S. B. in Sinigaglia à cauallo, doue fu incontrato da tre mila soldati tutti scielti, di buona presenza, e bene all'ordine, tutti con monitioni, & archibugi, & il restante con corsaletti, e picche, & erano vndici insegne, dapoi 24. giouani vestiti di raso bianco trinato d'oro, con bastoni inargentati in mano, e spade. & pugnali dorati, alla staffa di Sua Santità. In oltre, S. A. con molti principali Signori, Conti, Caualieri, & Capitani ricchissimamente adornati, andorno incontro à S B. cinque miglia, doue S. A. caualcaua sempre appresso Sua Santità, ouero solo inanzi. Di più, oltre all'apparato per tutte le strade della Città, vi era vn'arco fatto a dissegno, con statue finte di bronzo naturalissime, e motti bellissimi sopra la ricuperatione di Ferrara, e della beneditione del Rè di Francia; fù alloggiato nel palizzo di S. A. e si fece corte bandita molto copiosamente, dapoi furono fatti fuochi, razi, e tiri di molta Artiglieria in segno d'allegrezza: & erano preparate tre fregate armate di Sua Altezza, per andare a diporto per mare; le tre galere Venetiane sono sempre venute costeggiando sino à Sinigaglia, seguitando la Corte.

Sabbato Sua Santità andò ad alloggiare a Fano, oue fu riceuuto da 24. giouani vestiti di tabeto bianco fatto à onde, & vi erano molti archi.

Domenica mattina arriuò à Pesaro, & entrò à cauallo sotto vn bellissimo baldachino, doue fu riceuuto superbissimamente da S. A. sino a' suoi confini, e da cinquanta giouani vestiti ricchissimamente d'vn drappo col fondo d'oro, e furono fatti Archi, & apparati bellissimi, senza poi le militie, e superbissima caualcata di Signori, & Gentil'huomini, Gl'Illustriss. SS. Cardinali furono con bellissimo ordine mattina, e sera seruiti da gl'officiali di S. A. la quale mangiò con N. S. sola.

Lunedì sera S. S. arriuò a Rimini, doue fu riceuuta dalle militie, & da alcuni Caualli leggieri, e 40. fanciulli con oliua in mano vestiti di giallo, e turchino, & 25. giouani con le mazze in mano, non vi furono nè archi, nè apparati, ma solo vna fonte, che buttaua vin bianco, & il Sereniss. Sig. Duca di Modona arriuò quì, & cenò con Nostro Signore, tutti due soli.

Martedì mattina arriuò al Cesenatico, e da Monf. Dandino fu riceuuto nobilmēte Martedì sera à Rauenna, doue fu incontrato sù i confini da gl'Ambasciatori, e poi da diuersi Gentilhuomini a caua'lo, & in carozze, la militia, e 40. giouani vestiti di giallo turchino, e casacca di velluto negra, con archi motti, & apparati.

Mercordì passò per Bagnacauallo, Lugo, & Codignola.

ESSENDOSI hauuto auiso mercordì fera, 6. del prefente che la mattina feguente doueua giungere il fantiffimo Sacramento a S. Giorgio Chiefa poco fuori di Ferrara con belliffimo Conuento doue habitano i Monaci della Congregatione di Monte Oliueto, fù l'iftefla fera intimato alle confraternità de' Laici,& a tutto il Clero di andarlo à rincontrare, fi come poi fù fatto da tutti loro giouedì mattina (giorno folenne in Ferrara per effere la fefta di S. Maurelio Protettore della Città, & fanto di molta deuotione) portando ciafcuno, così confratri, come Frati, & Preti le torci in mano fmorzate, fin che rincontrato il Santiffimo Sacramento vn miglio di là da S. Giorgio le accelero, Mettendofi poi tutti in ordinanza andauano inanzi alcuni trombetti, & caualleggieri di N. Sig. Dopò i quali feguiuano le Confraternità di Laici, i Frati di diuerfe Religioni, i Parocchiani della Città,i Giouani del Seminario con le Cotte, i Canònici del Duomo, i cantori della Capella di N. Signore, i Trombetti della Città,due Mazzieri di S. Beatitudine con le loro mazze d'argento,& due Chierici della Capella di S. Santità con vn lanternone per ciafcun incima d'vn'hafte. Seguiua apprefo il fantiffimo Sacramento portato fopra vna chinea bianca condotta da due Palafrenieri di N.Sig.la quale haueua al collo vna campanella d'argento, & era ornata beniffimo con l'arme di fua Beatitudine & alle bande era guardia de Sguizzeri,fopra la fella della medefima chinea era vna caffetta coperta di broccato d'oro, dentro la quale era il fantiffimo Sacramento, & fopra la medefima caffetta era vn baldachinetto,tra il quale & la caffetta fi vedeua vna Croce d'oro d'altezza di vn palmo e mezo. Appfeffo il fantiffimo Sacramento feguiua Monfig. Sacrifta, & il compagno, & dopò effi dodeci Prelati. Gionti con quefto ordine alla porta della Chiefa di fan Giorgio alle 14.hore fu fubito leuato la fuddetta caffetta col fantiffimo Sacramento di fella della Chinea, & portata da alcuni delli fuddetti Padri fopra l'altare maggiore, cantandofi in tanto da i fuddetti Mufici l'hinno Pāge lingua gloriofa,&c. finito l'hinno fù letto vn breue di N.Sig.col quale fua Santità concede indulgenza à tutti quelli che accompagnano il fantiffimo Sacramento ò fi trouan prefenti quando viene portato nelle Chiefe. Per tutto quel giorno fù grandiffimo concorfo di gente à quella Chiefa, sì della Città, come foraftiera, che in gran quantità è venuta di Venetia, & fuo ftato, Bologna, Mantoua, & altri luoghi vicini.

L'iftefso giorno,fapendofi che N.Sig. con molti Cardinali doueua arriuare la fera, i Cardinali che erano giunti prima à Ferrara, gli Ambafciatori di Francia,& Venetia,molti Vefcoui,& altri, Prelati. alcuni Baroni Romani, tutti i Nobili,& molti altri Ferrarefi, & foraftieri andorno in diuerfe truppe à rincontrare N. Sig. il quale venne alla volta di S. Giorgio con quefto ordine;andaua innanzi à fua Santità vna compagnia di archibugieri à cauallo, & vna di caualleggieri della guarnigione di Ferrara,quefte fi erano inuiate la mattina per fare fcorta,& guida, feguiuano poi i Nobili, & altri Ferrarefi, foraftieri,alcuni cortegiani,la fameglia di N. Sig. i fudetti Baroni Romani,& il Crucifero

poi

Poi feguiua fua Santità in lettiga, & appreffo molti Cardinali, diuerfi Vefcoui
& Prelati à cauallo. Andauano dopò quefti tre altre compagnie di Caualleg
gieri, quella cioè del Monaldefchi, & le due ordinarie di N. Sig. Era concorfa
grandiffima quantità di popolo, sì della Città, come dello ftato, & foraftiero
a vedere fua Santità, la quale del continuo benediceua il medefimo popolo, &
concedeua anco Indulgenza alle corone di molti, che gli la dimandauano; nè
venne impedito alcuno dalla guardia di Sua Beatit. di farfi inanzi, & diman-
darli quello, che ciafcuno defideraua. Vicino fan Giorgio erano 500. foldati,
tra mofchettieri, & archibugieri diftefi alle bande. Giunto poi N. S. a fan Giorgio con buona, & allegra ciera alle 23. hore, fmontò di lettica, & entrato in
Chiefa andò a piedi fin'al faldiftoro, ch'era inanz il l'Altar maggiore, & ingi-
nocchiatofi con i Cardinali, & Prelati; mentre quefti fecero oratione al fantifs. Sacramento, furono da' Mufici della Capella refe gratie à Dio del felice
arriuo di fua Santità, fatto quefto S. B. licentiò i Cardinali, che tutti vennero
la fera ad alloggiare à Ferrara, & poi fi ritirò nel Conuento alle fue ftanze, che
fono le medefime doue alloggiò Papa Clemente 7. di fe. me. Doppò efferfi fua
Santità ritirata, li foldati, che erano alla guardia della porta di fan Giorgio, &
molti altri della guarnigione di Ferrara, che erano fopra la muraglia della città vicino alla detta porta fecero vna bella falua con li loro archibugi, & mofchetti, alla quale rifpofero li fudetti 500. foldati, & così fù fatto per tre volte;
poi li Bombardieri della medefima guarnigione, hauendo fatto condurre tutta l'Artiglieria di Ferrara fopra la muraglia fecero vn'altra belliffima falua, che
durò per vn pezzo, & fù tale lo ftrepito della medefima, che da molti anni in
quà non fe n'è vdita vna fimile.

Venerdì poi à 8. del prefente fua Santità diffe la meffa in fan Giorgio, doue
definò, & fi trattenne fino alle 21. hora, & effendo iui in tanto andati tutti i
Cardinali, Prelati, & altri, che fi diranno à i fuoi luoghi, fi auiorno tutti alla
volta della porta di fan Giorgio, andando N. S. à cauallo sù la mula fin'ad vna
ftanza fabricata di tauole, ornata di fiori, & frondi, & dentro di belliffime ta-
pezzerie, incontro la porta di fan Giorgio, che è ftata aperta hora nuouamen-
te, per occafione dell'ingreffo di fua Santità. Nella quale ftanza fua Beatitudine fi veftì pontificalmente, & in quel mentre fi cominciò l'ingreffo folenne
in Ferrara, con queft'ordine.

Andauano inanz i carriaggi di fua Beatitudine, cioè 85. muli, fopra ciafcuno de' quali era vna coperta di panno roffo con l'arme di fua Santità. Seguiuano poi due Corrieri, la Compagnia d'archibugieri à cauallo del Manti-
ca, la Compagnia di lancie del Monaldefchi, quella di lancie del Bufalo, quella
d'archibugieri del Iacouacci, & quella di lancie del Sig. Franciotto Orfino.
Doppò quefti feguiuano le ualigie pontificali de' Cardinali al numero di 27.
Altrettanti mazzieri de' Cardinali con le loro mazze, che pofauano fopra
gl'arcioni delle felle, 4. valigi Pontificali di N. S. dodici chinee bianche di
fua Santità, con belliffimi fornimenti, le quali erano menate a mano da dodici

dici Parafrenieri di fua Beatitudine, due lettiche di velluto cremefino, vna
fedia del medefimo velluto, portata da quattro parafienieri di fua Santità.
Seguiuano appreffo fei Trombetti a cauallo, i Caudatarij de' Cardinali, i Scudieri di N. S. le famiglie de' Cardinali, i Camerieri extra muros, tre Auocati
Conciftoriali, i Capellani fecreti, i Nobili Ferrarefi, & altri foraftieri nobiliffimamente veftiti, con ricche liuree, & belli caualli, alcuni Baroni Romani,
tre Auditori di Rota, i Camerieri fecreti, l'Ambafciatore di Bologna folo, &
li tre Ambafciatori di Francia, di Venetia, & Sauoia al pari, cioè quello di
Francia in mezo, quello di Venetia à man deftra, & quelle di Sauoia à man
finiftra. Dietro quefti andauano fei Trombetti di N. S. à cauallo, tutti i Preti,
& Monfignor Vefcouo di Ferrara à piedi, i Mazzieri di fua Santità con le loro
mazze d'argento a cauallo, due de virga rubea, il Crucifeto con la Croce di
fua Santità, due Chierici della Capella di fua Beatitudine con due lanternoni:
Seguiua poi il fantifs. Sacramento portato fopra la chinea, nel modo, che fi è
detto di fopra, nell'arriuo che fece a fan Giorgio, fotto vn baldacchino di rafo bianco, con l'arme del fantifs. Sacramento, il quale era portato da dodici
Sacerdoti. Dietro al fantifs. Sacramento andaua Monfig. Sacrifta, poi i Cardinali al numero di 27. à cauallo sù le mule pontificali, & doppò quefti Monfignor Theforiero generale, & vn parafreniero di N. S. con un baccile d'argento, nel quale erano le chiaui delle porte della Città, che dal Giudice de' Sauij erano ftate prefentate à fua Santità nella fudetta ftanza doue fi uefti pontificalmente. Seguiuano poi 30. Paggi, parte de' quali erano nobili, & parte
Gentilhuomini priuati, della città, veftiti tutti di tela d'argento, con berrette
di velluto negro, con treccie guarnite di rofette d'oro, perle, & gioie, con cap-
potti di velluto trinati d'argento, & foderati della medefima tela, con colla-
ne d'oro, & con fpade, & pugnali coi finimenti inargentati, fatti tutti à fpefe
proprie di ciafcuno. Veniua N. Sig. veftito Pontificalmente col Regno in tefta, di valore di mezo milione d'oro, portato fopra vna fedia da otto Parafrenieri, i quali haueuano le loro folite vefte roffe, fotto vn Baldachino di broccato d'oro col fondo roffo, & quefto era portato da i Dottori della città.
Intorno fua santità erano altri Parafrenieri, & dalle bande andaua la folita
guardia di Sguizzeri. Dietro s. B. erano alcuni Patriarchi, Arciuefcoui, Vefcoui, & altri prelati al numero di 40. à cauallo sù le mule pontificalmente: &
procedendo con quefto ordine entrorno per la fudetta porta noua di s. Giorgio, fopra la quale è ftata fatta dalla città un'arma di marmo di s. B. dalla parte
deftra l'arme del fig. Cardinale Aldobrandino, & dell'Eccellentifs. fig. Gio.
Francefco Aldobrandino, & dalla finiftra quelle dell'Illuftrifs. fig. Cardinale
s. Giorgio, & della città di Ferr. fotto la detta arma era la feguéte infcrittione,
Clemens V I I I. Pont. Max. Ferrariam bello Petri Aldobrandini Card. Im-
perio fœliciter gefto, atque incruenta prorfus victoria recuperatam, ingredienti
exultans fe cum in terris effe nactum Dominum, quo cœlum aperitur portam hanc
primam aperuit, Aldobrandinęque glorię æternum dicauit, popu. Ferrarien.
Anno Domini M D I I C.   Entrata

Entrata sua Beatitudine nella città, Monsig. Thesauriero generale comin‐
ciò à buttare al popolo de i danari à tutti i cantoni delle strade per doue pas‐
sò sua Santità le quali erano tutte adobbate con panni razzi, corami, altre
tapezzarie. & diuersi quadri di pittura, & alle finestre, ch'erano ornate di tap‐
peti, & drappi era concorsa gran quantità di Dame , & altre donne così della
città come forastiere, che faceuano bellis. vista. Vicino alla porta della Mon‐
tagna grande, per la quale strada si andò, era a man destra una bella prospettiua
sostenuta da quattro colonne di uerdura, con un quadro d'una donna turrita,
che daua mano ad un'huomo hirsuto appoggiato sopra un uaso, che non getta
acqua, figurato per il Pò asciuto. intorno le sorelle di Fetonte, sopra'l quadro.
Clem. V I I I. Pont. Max. Ferraria recuperata . con questi uersi .

Exanimum Clemens fluuiorum respice Regem,
Quo sine spes vitæ me quoque nulla fouet .
Hic me aluit genuitque illi da fundere limphas,
Viuere da nate posse parentis ope,
Sic armis quia victa tuis rediuiua vigebo,
ALDOBRANDINO Munere tuta pado.

A capo la strada della Giara, era un'altra prospettiua, con diuerse imprese di
guerra, col motto. Clem. VIII. P. M. Gloriosissi. ac prope diuinæ de Ferrariensi. bel‐
lo victoriæ, ex qua sine sanguine , sine dolo parta inter victorem, & victos specio‐
sum redintegratur certamen, hinc sinceri obsequij, inde paternæ beneficentiæ .
Su'l canto del saracino, doue si uoltò à man destra per andare da s. Francesco,
era un'altra Prospettiua, sostentata da 4. colonne, con l'arme di s. B. col motto.

Fœlix Bellum. Ex cuius semine destruentes rogo . Pax aurea in Ferrariensem
populum euolans suo occurrit Auctori, Clementi V I I I. Pont. Opt. Max.

Nella Giudecca al principio della strada di s. spirito era un'altra prospettiua,
con tre porte, con arme, angeli, & diuerse figure, & il motto.

Clem. V I I I. Pont. Max Clementiæ non inter innocentes, cessanti, sed fide, &
virtute lacescite; Ita omnibus succurrenti, vt ille omnibus venit .

In capo la strada della Giudecca à canto la fossa del castello era un'alta colóna,
simile à quella di Traiano, nella sommità della quale ui era una figura di don‐
na coronata, che tiene due corone nella mano sinistra, & nella destra un'ima‐
ginetta, figurata per la Gloria Aldobrandina. Di quà, & di là s. Pietro, & s. Pao‐
lo. Nella base della quale si leggono queste parole.

Clementis V I I I. Pont. Max. firmissimo monimento non titulorum saxis in‐
cisorum , sed solidissimæ internis animorum indiciis infixæ gloriæ.

Gionto N. Sig. in Duomo fece lunga oratione, & fatte le solite cerimonie si
spogliò gli habiti pontificali, & montò a cauallo per andare in castello al suo
alloggiamento, alla porta del quale staua il caualier Clemente capitano della
guardia, dal quale fu presentato le chiaui del castello à sua B. che per tenerezza
spargeua lagrime, mescolate con riso . così entrato dentro gli fu tolto la Mula
dal conte Romei, uno de i nobili detti di sopra, & s. santità andò à riposarsi.

NARRATIONE
DELLA SOLENISSIMA
ENTRATA IN FERRARA
DEL SERENISSIMO
DVCA DI MANTOA.

Et dell' Illustrissimi Ambasciatori di Venetia.

CON IL RECIVEMENTO
FATTOLI DA N. SIG. PAPA
CLEMENTE VIII·

Raccolto per Gieronimo Amarotti.

IN ROMA, Presso Bartholomeo Bonfadino. 1598
Con Licenza de Superiori.

Entrata dè Signori Ambasci-tori di Venetia.

Abbato che fù alli 30. di Maggio à hore ventitre fecero l'entrata l'Illustris simi Signori Ambasciato ri della Serenissima Signoria di Venetia, che furono con l'Assistente (che risiede appresso sua Santità) i,quali furono incontrati dua miglia lontani di Ferrara,da molti Prelati,li Caualli leggie ri,con la corte ordinaria di sua Santità,& dalla famiglia dell'Illustrissimi Cardinali secondo il solito che si vsa in Roma. Oltra che vi furono molti Gentill'huomini Ferraresi à Corteggiarli, & infinito Popolo, che iui concorse per vedere detta Entrata. I quali entrarono per la porta de gli Angeli, essendo accompagnati de cento Carozze da sei, & da quattro Caualli l'vna,& alloggiarono nel Monasterio di San Andrea.

Il giorno seguente che fù la Domenica alle 20.hore li sopradetti Signori Ambasciatori andorno con solenne pompa da sua Beatitudine all'audienza, (& iui sua Beatitudine li riceuerono con faccia allegra)bacciandogli li santissimi piedi,& di-

poi fecero la folita Oratione congratuſari
doſi dell'Augumento di ſanta Chieſa, dipoi ſi licentiorno, & ritornarono alla loro
habitatione.

Il Mercordì mattina che fù alli tre di
Giugno ſua Santità conuitò li ſopradetti
Ambaſciatori nella ſua ſtanza in vna Tauola poco diſcoſta da quella di ſua Beatitudine.

Entrata del Sereniſsimo Duca di Mantoua in Ferrara.

Iouedì che fù alli quattro di
Giugno arriuò tutti gli Officiali del ſereniſsimo Duca di
Mantoua, per mettere in ordine per il giorno ſeguéte, doue
fù apparecchiato vn bellifsimo & conde-
cente Palazzo, con bellifsime Tapezzarie
addobbato, con gran quantità di Canalli,
Corſeri, Chinee, Barbari, Gianetti, & Cur-
taldi, con bellifsime ſelle, e fornimenti recamati d'oro, & d'argento, di ſeta di diuerſi colori, con molta Vittouaglia per il vit-
to, e gran quantità de Vini, tenendo Corte bandita mentre che vi è ſtato.

Il giorno ſeguente arriuò il ſereniſsimo
Duca per il Pò, al Ponte Aucura diſcoſto
da

da Ferrara dua miglia, doue fù incontrato & riceuuto da dieci Illuſtriſsimi Cardinali, e da molti Prelati, & ſignori Ferrareſi con la Corte ſolita dell'Illuſtriſsimi Cardinali, & di molti Foraſtieri. L'illuſtriſsimi Cardinali fatte le ſolite accogliēze ſubito ſi partirno, & ritornorno alla Città.

A hore 2. cominciò auuiarſi la caualcata ſecondo l'vſo, in vn belliſsimo Prato, caſcando vn poco d'acqua minuta, che bagnaua li Pennacchi de' ſignori Mantoani, e Caſalaſchi, doue impediua quella belliſsima viſta, che ſaria ſtata ſe foſſe ſtato buō tempo. Arriuando alla porta de gl'Angeli doue ſtaua vna gran quantità de Soldati di ſua Santità in ordinanza con Picche, & Archibuſi, entrò detta Caualcata per la ſtrada de gl'Angeli, laquale era tutta piena di Gente, & tutte le fineſtre de' Palazzi erano adornati di belliſsimi drappi, ne' quali vi ſi appoggiauano belliſsime Dame, & Signore, facédo vna viſta mirabile.

In prima la Caualcata cominciò per detta ſtrada da' Caualli leggieri di ſua Santità, & innanzi vi era noue Trombette veſtiti di Liurea belliſsima di ſua Altezza, i quali faceuano vn'armonia di trombe belliſsima.

Dipoi ſeguiua i Paggi di ſua Altezza à Cauallo tutti veſtiti à Liurea.

Dipoi

Dipoi feguiua i Gentill'huomini mede-
fimamente fopra bellifsimi Caualii ric-
chifsimamente veftiti.

Appreffo vi veniuano li Cortegiani della Corte.

Dipoi feguiua i fignori Titolari Ferrarefi.

Dopo quefti feguiuano li fignori Mantoani, & di Cafale, con ricchifsimi veftiti
di diuerfi drappi, con oro, argento, & feta
recamati, con Capelli con trine d'oro maf
fiffo con Pennacchi con bellifsimi Gioielli
di grandifsima valuta, con Caualli bellifsi
mi, e felle con fornimenti ricamati d'oro
& d'argento, & ogn'vno di quefti Signori
haueua i fuoi Paggi, & Staffieri veftiti di
liurea di Velluto, & drappi di diuerfi colo
ri con bellifsimi ricami d'oro e di feta, qua
li Signori furono 54. con 54. forte di liurea.

Dipoi feguiua fua Altezza in vna Carozza di Velluto nero tirata da fei Caualli, la
qual era dell'Illuftrifimo Cardinale Aldo
brandino, & in detta Carozza, vi era con
fua Altezza fereniffima à canto à man finiftra Don Ferrante Gonzaga Prencipe
di Guaftala, e dietro loro era Monfignor
Matteucci, & Monfignor Gofredo, & all'in
contro di Don Ferrante, vi era il Prencipe di Maffa.

La Carozza era attorniata de Sguizzeri

ri della guardia di sua Santità, facendogli
spalliera di quà & di là, & attorno vi erano
molti Staffieri di sua Altezza, tutti vestiti
à liurea bellissima conueniente à vn tanto
Prencipe.

Appresso la Carozza seguiua tre bellissimi Caualli menati à mano, quali erano
per seruitio di caualcare per sua Altezza,
& erano adornati con fornimenti & sella
tutte recamate d'oro massissо, con molte
Gioie, Diamanti, Carboni, Rubini, Zafiri,
& Perle di grandissima valuta.

La Caualcata fù al numero di 400. Caualli con bellissimo ordine.

Dipoi seguirono 200. Carozze tutte tirate da sei, e da quattro Caualli l'vna.

Arriuò sua Altezza al Castello doue l'as-
pettaua sua Santità con gl'Illustrissimi
Cardinali, nella Sala Confistoriale, & arriuato smontò di Carozza, & s'ingenocchiò,
baciando i piedi à sua Beatitudine: & hauendo sua Santità fattolo leuare in piede
lo baciò ad ambedue le guancie stando à
man dritta di sua Santità con il Capello in
mano, fino à tanto che tutti quelli Signori
che erano có lui haueuano bacciato li piedi à sua Beatitudine, & subito fornito che
hebbero li detti Signori di bacciare i santissimi piedi, sua Beatitudine lo tornò ab-
bracciare, dipoi andò dall'Illustrissimi Car
di-

dinali facendo le folite Cerimonie fecondo l'vfo.

Fatte le Cerimonie fua Altezza fi partì, & andò al partamento che li fù confegnato per ordine di fua Santità (facendoli le fpefe à lui con 20. Gentil'huomini) & la fua Corte fe n'andò al fuo Palazzo. Et iui Don Ferrante Gonzaga ogni giorno mattina & fera dà da mangiare, à quanti Poueri vanno al fuo Palazzo.

Domenica che fù alli 24. di Maggio l'Illuftrifsima Signora Ambafciatrice di Spagna, con la moglie del fignor Haneo Pio, e la fignora Dona Marfifa Gentildonne Ferrarefe, andarono all'vdienza da fua Santità, doue furono riceuute gratifsimamente, & doppo hauere hauuto vdienza, d'ordine di fua Sàtità li fù apparecchiato vna collatione di Confettioni. Non altro pregato il fignor Iddio che ne cuftodifca nella fua gratia. Di Ferrara alli cinque di Giugno 1598.

LAVS DEO.

LA REALE
ENTRATA
Del Serenissimo
DVCA DI PARMA,
ET PIACENZA, &c.
IN FERRARA.

Descritta da D. Vincenzo Greco Catanese.

In Ferrara, Per Vittorio Baldini,
Stampatore Camerale.

ENTRATA IN FERRARA
DEL SERENISSIMO
DVCA DI PARMA,
& Piacenza , &c.

L Sereniſſimo Duca di Parma deſide-
roſo di paleſare al mondo la particu-
lare deuotione ſua verſo la Sede Apo
ſtolica , & la Santità di N. S. CLE-
MENTE VIII. ſi riſolſe li dì paſ-
ſati di venire à far riuerenza, & à ba-
ciare i piedi à Sua Beatitudine con
quella grandezza,& ſplendore ch'al-
lo ſtato, & all'animo ſuo ſi conueniua , nel che egli è ſtato
ſeruito dalla più parte de' ſuoi Feudatarij, e Caualieri, con
tanta affettione, & ſplendidezza , quanta ſi poteſſe deſide-
rar maggiore. Si che l'entrata ch'egli fece in Ferrara il dì
di S. Pietro fù vna delle coſe magnifiche , e preclare, che ſi
ſian viſte da molti anni in quà in Italia. Il che m'ha moſſo
a deſcriuerla con ogni breuità , acciò che la memoria d'vn
fatto coſi nobile, anzi heroico non periſca.

Douendo Sua Altezza partire il Sabbato dimandò il
Conte Carlo S. Vitale ſuo caualericcio maggiore con tutti
li ſtaffieri,& paggi , & vna parte della ſua famiglia, & robbe, dandoli per ſcorta cinquanta ſoldati, parte moſchettie-
ri , parte Archibugieri, & eſſendoſi partito il Sabbato medemo da Parma per le poſte, accompagnato dall'Illuſtriſſi-
mo Cardinale ſuo fratello, & da molti Caualieri de' ſuoi:
gionto all'imbarco trouò tutta la ſua nobiltà imbarcata ſo
pra quattro barche grande riccamente adornate , iui S. A.

montò

montò sopra il Buccentoro, oue erano cento Moschettieri per guarda. Caminauano auanti due barche per antiguardia con 25.Moschettieri per ciascuna, oltre le quali ve n'erano molt'altre da seruitio,& per retroguardia vna con 40. lancie spezzate, delle quali era Capo il Conte Galeazzo Scotto, ch'hauendo ogn'vna le loro insegne di varij colori sparsi per il fiume faceuano bellissima mostra, & licentiatosi poscia il Sig. Cardinale da S.A. col Vescouo d'Ortona à mare,col Vescouo di Piacenza, & Monsig. S.Vitale dalla bocca della Parma se ne tornò in Carozza indietro,& i medemi Moschettieri licentiatisi cō vna honoratissima salua lo salutorno. Vicino à Bresello fù incontrato dal Gouernatore di quel luogo con quantità de soldati in bellissima ordinanza dato gia ordine,che si sparassero da cento pezzi di Artiglieria, & quelli soldati quasi scherzando con i Moschettieri del Buccentoro à gara continuorno le loro salue per gran pezzo. Il Sabbato sera si fermò à Guastalla,& per esser l'hora tardi cenò nel Buccentoro allegrissimamente.

Domenica mattina destatosi à buon'hora s'auuiò verso Ostia sul Mantouano,& vdita Messa à Portiolo si compiacque di desinar quiui, & tanta fù l'abōdanza delle viuande, che delle lor reliquie restò per vn pezzo satolla tutta quella gente. Cōparso già l'istesso giorno il Sig. Cōte Vincentio Guerrieri Ambasciator dell'Altezza di Mantoua, ringratiādo il Sereniss.di Parma dell'Ambascieria prima fatta, & ch'hauesse sù quel stato quell'autorità li piacesse, & cō altre somiglianti essibitioni. Et doppò l'hauerli dato conto che'l suo Prencipe si trouasse à Venetia con gl'Illustriss.Sig.Cardinali Mont'alto, & del Monte, si licentiò come cōueniua.

La sera del medemo giorno si fermò alla Massa, oue Sua Altezza per suo essercitio smontò, & doppò d'essere andato vn buon pezzo à diporto rimontò nel Buccētoro cō singolarissimo

lariſſimo ſuo piacere. La mattina ſeguente gionto alla Stel
lata vdì Meſſa, & parendo à S.Altezza luogo aſſai ameno
l'Abbadia de Frati di ſan Benedetto preſſo l'argine del Pò,
volendo godere della libertà della Campagna in vn belliſ
ſimo boſchetto deſinò con 110. de' ſuoi Caualieri có molta ſua ſatisfattione, & il doppò deſinare i Moſchetticri cominciorno ancor eſſi con varie forme di ſcaramucciare, &
di battaglie a dar trattenimento à S. A. & vn popolo infinito concorſoui, nel che il Capitan Giacomo Guerini,

    L'Alfiere Gieronimo Zucchi,

    Il Capitan Pellegrino Biella, &

    Il Capitan Aurelio,   Come ſoldati molto
prattichi nell'eſſercitio della guerra, corriſpoſero piena-
mente all'eſpettatione, che s'hauea della loro diſciplina.
Verſo le ſedici hore S.Altezza ſi remiſe in viaggio verſo il
ponte di Lago ſcuro, doue ſmontato ritrouò pronti tutti li
Staffieri, & paggi de ſuoi Feudatarij, & Caualieri, inuia-
tiſi verſo l'Iſola doue era infinito numero de Signori particolari Ferrareſi: & iui Sua Altezza vn buon pezzo ſi trat
tenne mentre ſi daua ordine per la ſua entrata in Ferrara,
& in quel mentre andorno à incontrarlo gl'Illuſtriſsimi
Signori

Card. Priuli.	Card. Bandino.
Card. Borromeo.	Card. Gallo.
Card. Sforza.	Card. Arigone.
Card. Santi Quattro.	Card. D'Auila.
Card. Burgheſi.	Card. Ghiuara.
Card. Bianchetto.	Card. San Clemente.
Card. Verona.	Card. Matthei.

    L'Ambaſciator dell'Imperatore.

    L'Ambaſciator di Spagna.

    L'Ambaſciator di Francia.

L'Ambafciator di Venetia.
L'Ambafciator di Sauoia.
Il Sig. Marco Pio, & il Sig. Enea Pio.
Il Marchefe di Mefferano venuto poco innanzi a compire
con Sua Santità, e molti altri Vefcoui, & Prelati. In tanto
il Sig. Card. Aldobrandino ragguagliato dal Sig. Mario
Farnefe dell'arriuo di Sua Altezza li mandò incontro vna
Compagnia di Lancie, & poco doppo le andorno incontro Monfi. Matteucci, & Monfi. Conte Vefcouo d'Ancona
mandati da N. Sig. con vn'altra Compagnia di Lancie; &
perche gl'incontri furono numerofi cagionò, che entraffe
nella Città a xxiij. hore, oue non accade dire quanto piene
foffero le ftrade, & carichi i poggi, & le feneftre di gente
infinita, defiderofa di vedere non tanto la pompa, & lo
fplendore delle liuree, & de' veftiti, quanto la perfona di
Sua Altezza, non meno amata, ch'amabile da ogni forte
di perfone; Entrò poi vna Compagnia di Lancie, facendo ala dentro la porta della Città, finche foffero paffati
molti Caualieri Ferrarefi; Seguì poi vn'altra Compagnia
d'Archibugieri a Cauallo, & dietro a quelle altri partico-
ticolari Caualieri Romani in gran numero. Seguirono poi
i Trombetti di Sua Altezza, & dietro a loro i Feudatarij, &
Caualieri Parmeggiani, & Piacentini, tutti con loro Staffieri, & paggi innanti. Doppo quefti comparì Sua Altezza con vn veftito di rafo tanè tutto pieno di riccami d'oro,
e d'argento, riccio foprariccio guarnito di perle, & gioie,
con vn cappello il cui cinto, & piega era ornato di diaman
ti di grandiffimo valore, con vn groffo mazzo d'agieroni,
fopra vn cauallo Leardo Corfiero, con fella di velluto tanè, guarnita tutta di perle, & gioie di gran valuta, tra Monfignor Vicelegato di Ferrara, & Monfignor Matteucci.
Seguiuano poi Monfignor

Il

Il Patriarcha Biondi.   Monfig. Arçiuefcouo di Sorento.
Monfig. Dandino.   Monfignor Bonuifi.
Monfignor Lomellino.   Montignor Ferrero.
Monfignor S. Vitale.   Monfignor Sorbellongo.
Honorato della Guardia de' Suizzeri di N. S. feguiuano
doppo detti Prelati il Conte Carlo S. Vitale, & dietro à lui
tutti i Paggi, & Camarieri di S. A. à cauallo nobiliffimamē-
te. Veniua appreffo il Conte Galeazzo Scotto Capitano
delle Lancie fpezzate con tutti i fuoi, & dietro à lui vn'infi-
nità di Carozze tutte à fei caualli, fuor che alcune poche a
quattro. Et entrato in palazzo fù falutato con vna gran fal
ua di diuerfi pezzi, & di mofchetti, & introdotto da S. Beatit. li baciò i piedi, & con molta grauità, & gratia le efpref-
fe la diuotione dell'animo fuo verfo la Sede Apoftolica, &
le fece offerta della perfona, & di tutte le forze fue cō molta allegrezza, & fodisfattione di S. Santità. Furono anche
introdotti i SS. Caualieri della Comitiua di S. A. & fecondo, che baciauano i piedi ad vno ad vno ella ragguagliaua
Sua Santità de' nomi, & delle qualità loro moftrando in
ciò molta amoreuolezza verfo ciafcuno: & licentiatofi
poi da Sua Santità, menato a' fuoi alloggi in palazzo immediatamente S. A. fù à vifitare l'Illuftrifs. Sig. Cardinali
Aldobrandino, & S. Giorgio, quali di lì a poco verfo le due
hore di notte li refero amendue la vifita cō molte carezze.
Gl'habiti, e liuree de' Signori, che l'accompagnorno
per numero, & per ricchezze furono fuperbiffime, ne fi po-
trebbe facilmente dire qual foffe più riguardeuole la materia, ò l'artificio, la varietà, ò l'inuentione, la diuerfità
delle foggie, o de' colori: tanto è, che nè gl'occhi di quefto
popolo fi fatiano di mirarle, e rimirarle, nè le lingue di ce
lebrarle, & inalzarle.

Ordine

Ordine dell'Entrata in Ferrara.

Cinque Trombetti.

Prima fila Il Sig. Conte di S. Secondo . } con staffieri, e paggi. 28.
Il Sig. Conte Fortunato Cesis. }

II. Il Sig. Conte Ottauio Scotto . Il Signor Conte Hippolito Landi. il Sig. Conte Girolamo Angusciola .   21.

III. Il Sig. Conte Marc'Antonio Rangoni. Il Sig. Conte Gio. Battista Masi. Il Sig. Conte Pio Torelli.   14.

IIII. Il Sig. Gio. Battista Piombino . Il Sig. Caualier Barattiero. Il Sig. Tomaso Angusciola.   14.

V. Il Sig. Marc'Antonio del Bene . Il Sig. Gio. Francesco Tarascone. Il Sig. Ottauio Tarascone.   13.

VI. Il Sig. Capitan Giacomo Guerini . Il Sig. Capitano Pellegrino Bielli. Il Sig. Girolamo Zucchi.   . . .

VII. Il Sig. Marchese Cesare Scotto. Il Sig. Marchese di Val di Mozzola .   16.

VIII. Il Sig. Sforza Pallauicino . Il Sig. Conte Giulio Cesare Boschetti. Il Sig. Conte di Viarolo.   14.

IX. Il Sig. Pietro Maria Pauari. Il Sig. Marc'Antonio Barattieri. Il Sig. Aleßandro Giapponi. Il Sig. Caualiero Nicelli. 15.

X. Il Sig. Caualier Moisè Mosac . il Signor Ottauio Scudelaro. Il Sig. Oratio Bascialuppo. Il Sig. Copelina.   . . .

XI. Il Sig. Marchese Vrbano . il Signor Conte Federico Angosciola .   14.

XII. Il Sig. Conte Aleßandro Angosciola . Il Sig. Conte Galuano Angosciola. Il Sig. Conte Annibale Scotto.   17.

XIII. Il Sig. Caualier Paolo Tagliaferro . Il Sig. Giberto Toccolo. Il Sig. Capitano Hercole Caßola. il Sig. Oratio Linati. 10.

XIIII. Il Sig. Lodouico Marazzani . il Signor Caualier Pozzo. Il Sig. Giouanni Pellegrini Casati.   14.

XV. Il Sig. Gio. Battista Barattieri. Il Sig. Alfonso Angosciola. Il Sig. Gio. Bernardino Roleri.   14.

XVI. Il Sig. Conte Cosmo Masi. Il Sig. Preuosto Zoboli. il Sig. Girolamo Mascrimedico di S. A.

XVII. Il Sig. Conte Roberto Benzoni . Il Signor Conte Cristoforo Landi. il Sig. Scipione Rosa.   11.

XVIII. Il

Le cui Liuree diſtintamente per ordine ſi deſcriueranno.

In conclusione i Feudatarij furono 70. I Caualieri 40.

I caualli di rispetto condotti doi giorni prima dal Capitano Ottauio Scudelari,& menati a mano da huomini con veste lunghe fino à mezza gamba alla Turchesca   250.

Le Carozze di S. A. di stima furono due, vna fornita di velluto rosso, guarnita riccamente d'oro, l'altra di velluto nero guarnita del medemo; Tirate da caualli i più grossi, & belli, che si siano visti da gran tempo in quà.

Tra le selle se ne videro da cento riccamente lauorate in oro, & ricamate vagamente.

I Moschettieri di Sua Altezza   100.

I Caualli leggieri, & lancie spezzate   100.

Li Trombetti vestiti a Liurea di Scarlatto guarniti d'oro riccamente furono 8. dui tra gl'altri nell'artificio del suonare non la cedono a suonator che sia.

I Staffieri, & Paggi furono   760.

V'erano poi altri Camarieri, Officiali, ragazzi, & Seruitori d'ogni conditione in gran numero.

Oltre alla satisfattione data da S. A. nel rendere le visite, hà apportato allegrezza infinita a tutta questa Città, col comparire publicamente, con molta maniera, & gentilezza, con le Dame Ferraresi, & co' Signori, & con ogni sorte di persone: seruito da' suoi Feudatarij, & gentilhuomini, & da altri in tanto numero, che le contrade di questa Città, benche lunghissime, erano corte, & le strade, benche amplissime, anguste alle file de' caualli, & de' Caualieri.

Non parlo de' Banchetti fatti a queste Signore, & Signori nella Città, & nel Buccentoro, nè delle Tauole mantenute sempre piene a poueri, nè della copia delle vettouaglie, & viuande per non passar il segno della breuità prescritta.

IL FINE.

RELATIONE

Dell'entrata solenne fatta in Ferrara à dì 13. di Nouembre 1598.

PER LA SERENIS. D. MARGARITA D'AVSTRIA
Regina di Spagna: Et del Concistoro publico con tutti li prepa-
ramenti fatti dalla Santità di N. S. CLEMENTE
PAPA VIII. per tal'effetto.

Con minuto raguaglio della Messa Pontificale cantata da S. Beatitudine,
delle ceremonie delli sposalitij fatti nella Chiesa Cathedrale di detta
Città Domenica alli 15. del medesimo, con la ceremonia della
Rosa, che S. S. finita la messa donò alla Regina.

*Descritta da Gio. Paolo Mocante, vno de' Maestri di ceremonie della
Cappella di S. Beatitudine.*

Ad instanza di Ottauiano Gabrielli.

In ROMA, Appresso Nicolò Mutij. M. D. XCVIII.
Con licenza de' Superiori.

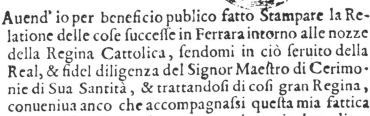

ALL'ILLVSTRISS. SIG.
IL SIGNOR D. THOMASSO
D'AVALOS D'ARAGONA,

Signor, & Patrone mio Col.^{mo}

Auend'io per beneficio publico fatto Stampare la Relatione delle cose succeffe in Ferrara intorno alle nozze della Regina Cattolica, fendomi in ciò feruito della Real, & fidel diligenza del Signor Maeftro di Cerimonie di Sua Santità, & trattandofi di cofi gran Regina, conueniua anco che accompagnafsi quefta mia fattica con perfona di Authorità, alla quale anco per mia particolare diuotione mi fofsi già vn pezzo fà dedicato fideliffimo Seruitore qual è, V. S. Illuftriff. come Signore di nobiliffimo Sangue, & Nipote dell'Illuftriffimo & Reuerendiffimo Legato di Roma, cofi gran Cardinale, che con tanta prudenza hà gouernato, & gouerna queft'Alma Città, oltre le rare qualità di V. S. Illuftriff. alla protettione della quale in tutto mi dono, fupplicandola con ogni affetto a non fdegnarfi di abbracciar cofi picciol dono, ma riceuendolo con la fua folita humanità rifguardar il fuifcerato animo mio verfo V. S. Illuftriff. a cui pregando da Dio il colmo d'ogni felicità e contento humilmente le faccio riuerenza.

Di V.S. Illuftrifsima.

Humiliffimo, & Diuotiffimo Seruitore

Ottauiano Gabrielli.

RELATIONE

Dell'entrata folenne fatta in Ferrara à di 13. di Nouembre 1598.
per la Sereniſsima Margarita d'Auſtria Regina di Spagna,
& del Conciſtoro publico con tutti li preparamenti
fatti dalla Santità di N. S. Clemente Papa
Ottauo per tal'effetto.

ON ſi potria dire con quanto deſiderio la Santità
di N. S. CLEMENTE Papa Ottauo habbia
aſpettato, & con quanta allegrezza poi riceuuto
in Ferrara la Sereniſima Regina Margarita d'Auſtria nouella ſpoſa della Sac. Reg. Cattolica Maeſtà
di Filippo III. Rè di Spagna. Poiche molti giorni
prima, che arriuaſſe mandò fino in Terra Tedeſca
Monſ. Mattheucci Arciueſcouo di Raguſa, & Veſcouo di Viterbo Prelato digniſsimo, & familiare
di S. Santità à viſitarla, & incontrarla, & ſubito
che inteſe, che ſi auuicinaua verſo Italia gli mandò incontro l'Illuſtriſsimo, &
Reuerendiſsimo S. Cardinale Aldobrandino ſuo nipote. Et per honorare la
venuta ſua, & riceuerla con quel maggior honore, che fuſſe poſsibile non hà
perdonato à ſpeſa, ne ha laſciato in dietro coſa alcuna, che ſi ſia poſſuta fare
da vn ſanto, pio, & diuoto Pontefice in honore di vna così gran Regina, che
ſi può dir, che ſia, & ſenza dubio è la maggiore del mondo. Et laſciando da
parte li nobili, & ſontuoſi apparecchi, & preparamenti di vettouaglia, li belliſsimi preſenti, che haueua apparecchiati per donarli, li adornamenti, & ad-
dobbaméti delle ſtanze, la noua liurea, della quale S. Santità con queſta occa-
ſione ha fatto riueſtire tutte li ſuoi Palafrenieri ſontuoſiſsimamente con cap-
potti, & colletti di veluto nero, calzoni di velluto cremoſino, & giupponi di
raſo del medeſimo colore, & molte altre coſe, che non appartengono all'officio, & profeſsion mia, & delle quali io non poſſo dar quella intiera, & vera
relatione, che conuerria, dirò ſolamente alcuna coſa con breuità dell'adornamento delle ſtanze preparate per S. Maeſtà, della ſala grande del Conciſtoro
publico, dell'adornamenti della Chieſa Cathedrale doue furon fatti li ſponſalitij, delli archi & inſcrittioni, della magnifica, & ſontuoſa entrata di S. Maeſtà
in Ferrara, del Conciſtoro publico, & finalmente della Meſſa cantata da Sua
Beatitudine, & ceremonia fatta in Chieſa per li ſponſalitij, & della Roſa, che
S. Santità donò finita la Meſſa alla Regina.

Le ſtanze, che furono aſſegnate per S. Maeſtà ſtanno nel palazzo contiguo,
& attaccato al caſtello di Ferrara, doue habita Sua Beatitudine, che rieſcono
da vna banda verſo la Peſcaria, & dall'altra verſo vn giardino, & cortile
grande del Palazzo, & alle quali da quelle di S. Santità per vn'iſteſſo piano col
mezzo di alcuni ponti leuatori ſi può andare, & tutte furono adornate nobi-

liſsi-

lifsimament e di panni di razza belliſſimi, ma principalmẽte la prima ſala
grande, qual e fù adorna delli più belli, & ricchi panni di razza, che ſi poſſano
deſiderare, n on ſolo per la materia, eſſendo tutti inteſſuti non di altro che di
ſeta, argento, & oro; ma per le mirabili, & artificiuſe figure, & diſſegni, che
vi ſono, nell i quali ſi vedeua inteſſuta, & ritratta con figure belliſſime, che
pareuano viue tutta la hiſtoria della creatione del mondo deſcritta da Moiſe
nel principio del Geneſi. La ſtanza poi, ò camera ſeguente era adorna di paramenti di velſuto cremoſino, guarniti con belliſſime, & ricchiſſime trine di
oro,& nobil fregio da capo, con ſedie, & altri adornamẽti del medeſimo. L'anti
camera poi della Regina fù adornata di certi drappi inteſſuti con ſeta bianca,
verde, roſſa, & oro, ne'quali ſi vedeuano certi fogliami, & grappi d'vua, che
faceuano vna nobiliſſima viſta, con vn baldachino ricchiſſimo d'oro lauorato
all' Indiana, & con portiere ſimili, & ſedie, & fornimenti neceſſarij. Ma la camera iſteſſa della Regina doue haueua da dormire S. Maeſtà, con il letto, ſedie, & ogni altro adornamento,& guarnimento neceſſario fù di nuouo à queſto effetto fatta guarnire, & ornare da S. Santità di nuoui paramenti di broccato in campo roſſo, & tela di argento, vna colonna dell'vno, & vna dell'altro drappo, con ſedie del medeſimo broccato, baldachino, letto, tauolino,
inginocchiatore, & ogni altra coſa neceſſaria del medeſimo adorni con trine,
& frangie d'oro. Nella retrocamera poi vi era vn ſuperbiſſimo letto, con vn
cortinaggio di broccato riccio ſopra riccio, con lauori all'Indiana, & tutta la
ſtanza era guarnita nobiliſſimamente di paramenti di broccato, con vn tauolino di argento, focone, ſpechiera, & altre coſe neceſſarie per le dame, che io
non ſò, ne poſſo hora riferire.

La ſala poi del Conciſtoro publico doue S. Santità nel primo arriuò haueua
da riceuere la Regina, che fu vn ſalone grandiſſimo che rieſce nel cortil grande doue ſuol ſtare la guardia de ſoldati, nel quale ſoleua la bon. mem.del Duca
Alfonſo fare li torneamenti, & altre feſti in Ferrata per eſſer loco capaciſſi-
mo, & grande di longhezza oltre ducento palini, & di larghezza circa ottanta
fù nobiliſſimamẽte adornata. Et ſe bẽ per andare à detto Salone vi erano ſcale
da più bande, nondimeno per honor della Regina fù fatta vna nuoua ſcala nel
cortile che à punto riuſcina auanti la porta Maggiore di detto Salone con ſet-
tanta ſcalini piaceuoli, ciaſcuno alto poco meno di mezo palmo, & lunghi cir
ca quattordici palmi, à piedi della quale furono poſte due ſtatue finte di marmo bianco, cioè quelle di San Pietro & di San Paolo Principi delli Apoſtoli,
vna dalla deſtra, & l'altra dalla ſiniſtra. Et fù adorno detto Salone di nobiliſſi-
mi panni di razza inteſſuti fimilmente con ſeta, & oro, nelli quali con mirabil
artificio, & belliſſime figure ſi vedeua tutta l'iſtoria di Gioſeppe deſcritta ſimilmente da Moiſe nel Geneſi cominciando al capit. 37. In capo di detta ſala
fù accomodato il Solio & Sedia del Papa al quale ſi aſcendeua per ſette ſcalini
alti poco più di mezo palmo l'vno, quali di mano in mano ſi veniuano reſtrin-
gendo in ſù, in maniera che eſſendo il primo lungo, ò per dir meglio largo circa 40. palmi, l'vltimo doue ven ua ad eſſere il piano del ſolio era largo 24. pal
mi, & lungo 12. (perche io piglio, & chiamo la lunghezza del Solio per il mede
ſimo

fimó verfo della lunghezza della fala) fù parato detto Solio con tutti li fcalini di panno roffo,& vi fù pofta vna Pôtificale fedia di Sua Santità adorna di broc cato roffo fotto al baldacchino,& nel piano della fala con vguale,& proportio niata diftanza furono pofti,& ordinati li banchi per l'Illuftriff. & Reuerendiff. Signori Cardinali coperti di panni di razza,& il piano della quadratura fu tut to coperto di panni verdi.Et perche fi dubitaua che il Conciftoro publico per il riceuiméto della Regina poteffe arriuare alla notte, furono preparate fede ci torciere,che dal foffito di detto Salone con corde furono calate a baffo, ac ciò bifognando fi illuminaffe la fala,& in ciafcheduna torciera erano quattro torcie bianche; & perche quefto haueua da effere vn Conciftoro non come gli altri ordinarij,volfe Sua Santità,che vi fuffe anco qualche cofa di eftraordina rio,cioè vn palco per li mufici, accioche, mentre fi rendeua l'obedienza, & al venire & partire della Regina fi fentiffe qualche armonia fuaue : & fu acco modato detto palco per li cantori & Mufici di S. Santità fopra la porta gran de di detto Salone.

La Chiefa poi Cathedrale di Ferrara dedicata alli Gloriofi Santi Giorgio, & Maurelio Martiri,nella quale S.Santità haueua da cantare la meffa folenne per il giorno del Spofalitio, fù adornata & parata nobiliffimamente meglio che mai fia ftata parata, & adorna in alcun'altro tempo ; & acciò che il luogo della Cappella fuffe più commodo,& capace,fu fatto vn palco al paro del Pref biterio,& Croce della Chiefa alla quale fi afcédeua per 9.fcalini,& arriuò det to palco fin all'organo,& quanto teneua tutto l'arco doue fta detto organo, & era detto palco & piano della cappella dal principio fino al Solio del Papa lun go circa palmi cento, & largo poco meno di cinquanta. L'altare fu pofto in mezo con tre gradili fotto, & fu accommodato nella maniera,che fta l'altare di San Pietro in Roma.Il Solio,& Sedia del Papa fu pofta incontro à detto alta re & à punto nel luogo doue fuole ftare l'altare maggiore ordinario di detta Chiefa, fù fatto intorno intorno per quanto teneua il luogo della cappella vn riparo di tauole per reprimere la moltitudine del popolo che vi farebbe con corfo, & hauerebbe occupato ogni cofa non baftando in fimile occafione ne guardie de foldati, ne altre ordinarie diligenze, & vi fù lafciata aperta fe non vna porta per doue s'haueua da entrare alla cappella, & cò tutto quefto vi en trò poi tanta gente che con difficultà poteuano li miniftri far l'officio loro per la cappella,come appreffo fi dirà,Ma non fi potè fare altro, per rifpetto de foraftieri,& moltitudine di popolo che era concorfo in Ferrara per quefta oc cafione, Onde non baftando li palchi fatti nel vano della Croce della Chiefa fuori della quadratura,che pur vi era rimafto loco capace per molto popolo, entrorno ancora molti infieme col Papa,& con i Cardinali dentro la quadra tura, oltre che tutta la Chiefa da ogni banda fi empì di popolo infinito.

Fù adorna la Chiefa ch'è grande & capace tutta di belliffimi panni di raz za,& tra gli altri ve n'erano alcuni,nelli quali era dipinta l'hiftoria delli Glo riofi Santi Giorgio & Maurelio padrone & Aduocati di Ferrara . Ma tùtta la Croce del Presbiterio,& per quanto fi vedeua intorno intorno dal piano del la cappella fu adorna parte di belliffimi panni di razza di S. Santità nelli qua

ì erano inteffute diuerfe hiftorie facre del teftamento nuouo, & parte di pa-
liotti di damafco con fioroni d'oro di diuerfi colori che fi adoprano per ferui-
tio delle cappelle li quali alternatamente tra vn panno di razza . & l'altro con
bella & elegante propofitione furno accomodati in maniera, che faceuano bel
lifsima moftra . Sopra li quali fu fatto vn fregio che circondaua non folo
detta Croce della Chiefa intorno intorno, & per quanto teneua il piano della
cappella, ma anco tutta la naue grande di mezzo della Chiefa nel qual fregio
che fù adornato di feftoni, & fioroni rofsi con eguale, & proportionata diftanza furono dipinte, & pofte tutte l'arme dell'Illuftriff. & Reuerédiff. Signori Car
dinali, che hoggi viuono, & fopra le due colonne, ò pilaftri che foftentano la
volta della tribuna di qua, & di là furono pofte due grandifsime arme del Papa
& poi a man dritta cominciaua l'arme del Signor Cardinal Gefualdo Decano
del Sac. Collegio, & à man manca quella del Signor di Aragona Vefcouo di
Porto, & cofi di mano in mano con eguale, & bella diftintione feguitauano tut
te l'altre armi de Signori Cardinali viuenti, & nelli nicchi che fofteneuano, le
volte, & colonnate della Chiefa nel medefimo ordine, & fregio tra le armi de'
Cardinali erano pofte, doue l'imagine di San Giorgio, doue quella di San Mau
relio, & doue l'arme della Chiefa con giufto & eguale compartimento . Fuori
fopra la porta Maggiore della Chiefa fu pofta vna grande arme del Papa, &
dalle bande di quà, & di là due armi grandi della Chiefa con le chiaui, & vm-
brella. Sopra la porta minore à man dritta furono pofte due altre arme grandi cioè quella del Rè, & della Regina, & fopra la porta della Chiefa à man man
ca furono pofte due altre arme fimili vna dell'Arciduca, & l'altra dell'Infante.
Scontro la porta maggiore della Chiefa auanti all'arco che riefe nel cortile
grande del Palazzo doue era la fcala per afcendere al Salone del Conciftoro ,
fu fatto vn bellifsimo arco trionfale figurato di marmo Africano con quattro
colonne fimili due per banda, & in mezo à dette colonne dall'vna, & l'altra ban
da era vn nicchio , nel quale fu pofta vna ftatua per banda finta di marmo
bianco, che rapprefentauano (come io credo) doi donne che fecondo l'vfo de
gli Antichi Romani, chiamauano Himeneo con vna face di pino accefa in mano, vna con la tefta coronata di vna fronda che chiamano Amaraco. Et fopra
la ftatua dalla banda dritta era con lettere maiufcole fcritto I VGVM. Et fopra la ftatua della banda finiftra era fcritto MARITALE.
    In cima di detto arco furono pofte tre armi grandi, cioè quella del Papa in
mezzo, quella del Rè à man dritta, & quella della Regina à man manca; & dalle bande di quà , & di là quafi in cima dell'arco erano due ftatue finte ti marmo bianco con le ali, & con vna tromba in bocca figurata per la fama. Et fotto
lle predette armi del Papa, Rè , & Regina nel frontifpitio del Arco con lettere maiufcole fi leggeua la feguente infcrittione, cioè.

    Philippo, & Margarita Auftriacis.
    O vita Jmperatorum gloria fuaque pietate inclitis.
    Vt Catholicorum Regum foboles propagetur

                                                        Matrimo.

Matrimonio diuinitus coniunctis
Anni multi, liberorum copia, perpetua fœlicitas.

Furono poi di ordine di Superiori fatte nettare tutte le ſtrade per doue haueua da venire la Regina, ſe ben dopoi per riſpetto di vna pioggia che venne
il giorno auāti à quello dell'entrata ſi erano di nuouo imbrattate, & furono fat
ti diuerſi ponti di nuouo nelli paſsi cattiui dall'Iſola luogo di doue ſi haueua
da partire la Regina il giorno dell'entrata fino in Ferrara.

La porta della Citta per doue ſi haueua d'entrare che fu quella delli Angio
li dalla banda di fuori fu dipinta, & adorna con tre armi, cioè del Papa, del Rè,
& della Regina, & con la ſeguente inſcrittione ſotto.

Angeli gaudent; Mortales exultant Margaritam.
Auguſti ſanguinis pietatis, virtutumque omnium ſplendore luci-
diſſimam.
Simul lætiſſimè excipiunt.

Et dalla banda di dentro fu adorna con cinque arme cioè quella del Papa in
mezo, quella del Rè alla ſua deſtra, & quella della Regina alla ſiniſtra, & appreſſo à quella del Rè l'arme dell'Arciduca, & appreſſo quella della Regina l'-
arme dell'Infante, & ſotto vi furono ſcritte quelle lettere.

Urbem aduentus tui lumine Jlluſtratam Regina.
Redde nunc hoſpitio glorioſam.

Auuicinandoſi il tempo della venuta di S. Mieſtà, la Santità di N. S. dopò
il Conciſtorio publico fatto nel Caſtello nella ſala che ſtà auanti la ſua buſſola
per la venuta dell'Illuſtriſſ. & Reuerendiſſ. Signor Cardinale di Fiorenza, che
torno dalla ſua legatione di Francia martedi alli X. del preſente meſe di Nouembre, creò doi legati di latere per andare jncontro alla Regina fino all'Iſola, & queſti furono l'Illuſtriſſ. & Reuerendiſſ. Signori Cardinali Bādino & San
Clemente. Et ſi aſpettaua che Sua Maeſtà doueſſe arriuare all'Iſola il mercordì ſera alli xj. & ſi credeua che doueſſe far l'entrata giouedì alli xij. ma poi fù
differita per il giorno ſeguente che fù venerdì alli xiij. del medeſimo.

Et perche anco all'Iſola foſſe la Regina riceuuta, & honorata, come ſi conue
niua, deputò S. Santità doi Prelati delli ſuoi aſsiſtenti cioè Monſignor Conte
Veſcouo di Ancona, & Monſignor Viſconte Veſcouo di Ceruia, che andaſſero
all'Iſola predetta che è vn luogo aſſai bello del Duca di Modona, diſcoſto da
Ferrara circa tre miglia à preparare, & ordinare tutte le coſe neceſſarie per
il biſogno di S. Maeſtà in quel luogo doue haueua da fermarſi vna ſera, & deſinare il giorno ſeguente. Onde furono le ſtanze di detto luogo adornate nobiliſſimamente, & vi fù preparato ogni coſa neceſſaria, coſi per dormire, come
per mangiare con abondanza, & magnificenza.

Arriuò la Regina inſieme con l'Arciducheſſa ſua Madre, & con l'Arciduca
Alberto ſuo Cognato il giouedì ſera in detto luogo, doue da vn buccentoro
del

del Duca di Modona, doue fopra il quale per il Pò era venuta accompagnata da molte altre barche difcefe. Et prima che sbarchaffe iui arriuò l'Illuftriff.& Eccellentiff. Signor Cio. Francefco Aldobrandino Capitan Generale di Santa & nipote di S. Santità con bella compagnia di Gentilhuomini, & con l'Illuftrif fimo Signor Siluefro Aldobrandino fuo figliuolo & con la guardia di Cauall-leggieri di S.Beatitudine, & tutti li foldati à cauallo che fi trouano al prefente in Ferrara, & fatta che hebbe riuerenza à S. Maeftà.& all'Arciducheffa, & Ar-ciduca,& falutatili à nome di S. Beatitudine,fe ne tornò in dietro, & arriuò à Ferrara ad vn'hora di notte in circa,

Tutto quel giorno del gioue di entrorno in Ferrara molti Tedefchi, & altre perfone della famiglia di S. Maeftà,& delli Sereni ſimi Signori Arciducheffa, & Arciduca,& il fimile fece tutto il giorno feguente cominciando della mat-tina à buon'hora che introrno fempre diuerfe perfone,muli, carriagi.& robbe di detti Sereniſimi Principi.

Il giorno deputato per l'entrata che fu venerdì alli 13. di Nouembre li doi fopradetti Illuſtriſsimi Cardinali Bandino, & San Cleméte Legati de latere di S. Santità con bella,& fontuofa compagnia de Gentilhuomini à cauallo verfo 17. hore s'inuiorno all'Ifola per trouare la Regina, & vn mezzo miglio fon-tano dal luogo predetto,doue S. Maeftà fi era fermata, venne incontro alle Si-gnorie loro Illuſtriſsime,Il Sereniſsimo Alberto Arciduca d'Auftria à cauallo, con nobil compagnia di Signori,& Gentilhuomini tutti veftiti di nero, & Mó figner Vifconte Vefcouo di Ceruia venne vn poco innanzi à dire all'Illuftriſsi mi Legati,che S. A. li veniua incontro,& defideraua fapere fe le Signorie loro Illuftriſsime voleuano che fi fmontaffe,ò pure fi contentauano che fi faceffero li complimenti à cauallo,& li Legati fi rifolfero di farli à cauallo. Cofi quando furono vicini l'Arciduca fe fece incontro alli Legati,& li falutò con parole pie ne di amoreuolezza,& cortefia,& hauuta la rifpofta da loro,& fatte infieme le debite confalutationi, caualcorono verfo l'Ifola, doue afpettaua la Regina tutti tre à vn paro,effendofi meffo l'Arciduca nel luogo più infimo,cioè alla fi-niftra del Cardinal Bandino, dalla cui deftra, caualcaua il Cardinal San Cle-mente. Arriuati che furono all'Ifola fmontorno tutti da cauallo, & andorno verfo le ftanze doue afpettaua la Regina,con l'Arciducheffa fua Madre,la qua le hauuto auuifo, che li Cardinali Legati erano già arriuati, fe leuò da federe dalla fedia, doue appreffo la Madre fedeua,& venne incontro alli Legati fino à meza ftanza, & in piedi afcoltò le parole che diffe il Cardinal Bandino dell'al-legrezza che haueua S. Santità della venuta di S. Maeftà,& come haueua man dato loro à riceuerla,& falutarla.

La Regina rifpofe alcune parole in lingua Tedefca, accennando ad vn Ve-fcouo che era feco,che refpondeffe in nome fuo alli Legati. Il qual riferito che hebbe prima alla Regina in lingua Tedefca, la foftanza di quello che haueua detto il Cardinal Bandino,& hauuta poi la commiffione da S. Maeftà rifpofe per lei alli Legati in lingua latina. Et fempre mentre fi fecero quefti compli-menti ftettero tutti in piedi. Dopoi la Regina con la Madre andorno à federe, in certe fedie baffe che ftauano fotto ad vn baldacchino in vn canto di detta
ftanza

ranza,& li due Legati federonò in due fedie Camerali fcontro la Regina, & l'-
Arciduca anchora fedè in vn'altra fedia al par loro, ma nel lnogo meno de-
gno cioè alla finiftra di Bandino.

Dopò che furono ftati vn pezzo à federe, & à ragionare co'l mezzo dell'interprete effendo già hora di auuiarfi verfo Ferrara fi leuò la Regina, & fu accompagnata dalli doi Cardinali Legati fino ad vna bellifsima carrozza di
velluto cremofino tutta guarnìta d'oro con fei bellifsimi cauaili, & doi cocchieri veftiti della medefima liurea. Nella quale erano due fole fedie quale
carrozza fu mandata à donare à S. Maeftà da N. Signore. Et entrata, che fu la
Regina in detta carrozza infieme cò la madre, li doi Cardinali Legati entrorno in vn'altra carrozza,& le fue vénero inanzi,& fi fermorono in vn luogo deputato nel prato difcofto dalla porta della Città forfe vn quarto di miglio, doue fu fatto à pofta vn cafone di legno, che dì détro fu tutto parato,& adorno,
nel quale fi fermorno li doi Cardinali Legati, & iui depofti li habiti corti dà
caualcare prefero le fottane lunghe rofse, & li rocchetti, & la cappa pauonaz-
za, & afpettorno che veniffe la Regina, la quale montata in carrozza con la
Madre fi auuiò pian piano verfo la città accompagnata da molti nobili Baroni,& Signori titulati con infinito numero de Gentil' huomini, & fuoi cor-
teggiani tutti veftiti di nero, & Sua Maeftà ancora era di nero veftita. Et per
antiguardia li andauano innanzi due fquadre di foldati à cauallo,vna di cauallegieri tutti armati con fopra vefti, & banderole negre, & vn'altra di archibugieri con fopra vefti nere con morrioni neri, & con certi accette, ò fecure
all'arcione. Auanti la carrozza di S. Maeftà caualcauano immediatamente
l'Arciduca Alberto in mezo tra il Duca di Seffa Ambafciator di Spagna, & il
Contestabile Gouernatore di Milano,dietro la carrozza della Regina veniuano circa altre fei carrozze di dame, & poi vna fquadra de arcieri dell' Arciduca tutti veftiti di nero.

Venne incontro à S. Maeftà fino all'Ifola il Sig. Pietro Aldobrandino Luo-
gotenente dell'Illuftrifs. Sig. Gio. Francefco, con tutti li caualli leggieri del
Papa, li quali poi che hebbero incontrata la Regina fe ne tornorno in dietro,
& fi auuiorno innanzi verfo Ferrara. Poco prima che la Regina arriuaffe al fopradetto cafone, li vennero incontro circa quattordici, ò fedici Prelati afsiftenti di S. Santità nell'habito pontificale con mantelloni, mule, & cappelli
pontificali mandati incontro à S. Maeftà dal Papa, li quali fatte due àle falu-
torno la Regina, & poi caualcorno appreffo à Lei, & alle fue Dame, & afpettorno fino che la Regina fmontò di carrozza, & entrò in detto cafone, doue
erano preparate due chinee con felle di donna, vna bianca guarnìta di tela
d'argento con trine d'oro per la Regina donatali da S. Santità, & vn'altra
per l'Arciduchezza guarnìta di valdrappa, & fornimenti di velluto pauonaz-
zi. In tanto effendofi fparati alcuni pezzi di artiglierie fi diede fegno al Sacro Collegio dell'Illuftrifsimi, & Reuerendifsimi Signoti Cardinali,che ve-
niffero incontro alla Regina, li quali afpettauano nel Conuento, & Chiefa di
Santa Maria delli Angioli, che è circa vn quarto di miglio lontano dalla porta della Città, & montati à cauallo fopra le loro mvle pontificali con cappe

B   pauo-

pauonazze andando prima le loro valigie, & immediatamente auanti le Signorie loro Illustrissime li Mazzieri con le Mazze alzate, accompagnati da vna nobil compagnia de gentil'huomini caualcarono verso la porta, & questi furono diecisette Cardinali, perche di venti, che si trouauano in Ferrara, l'Illustrisimo Cardinal Parauicino per vna sua indispositione non vi potè venire, & l'Illustrissimi Bandino, & S. Clemente erano già con la Regina. Quelli che vi vennero furono l'Illustris., & Reuerend.SS.Card.cioè di Fiorenza, Ascoli, Camerino, Montelparo, Giustiniano, Borromeo, Baronio, Bianchetto, Auila, Genara, Arrigone, Sforza, Montalto, Farnese, Santi Quattro Aldobrandino, & Cesis. Come si auuicinorno alla porta la Regina montò sopra detta chinea, & caualcando in mezo alli doi prefati Cardinali Legati venne verso la Città, & dietro di lei immediatamente caualcaua l'Arciduchessa sua madre à man diritta con l'Arciduca Alberto à man manca, & poi le dame della Regina, & li Prelati afsistenti come ho detto di sopra. Il Collegio de Cardinali vscì fuori della porta, & passati tutti li ponti si fermò aspettando la Regina, che pian piano caualcando li venne incontro, & arriuati che li hebbe, il Cardinal di Florenza(come il più vecchio)à nome di tutti gli altri salutò la Regina, & fece li soliti complimenti di parole per tutti, & perche S. Maestà non intendeua la lingua Italiana, rispose per lei l'Arciduca Alberto, & all'hora li doi Cardinali Legati hauendo finito la lor Legatione, lasciorno la Regina in mezo tra li doi primi Diaconi, cioè Sforza, & Montalto, & loro caualcorno con li altri nel luoco della loro promotione.

Nell'entrar, che fece la Regina in Ferrara apparue il Sole, che tuto quel giorno era stato nuuoloso, se bene non haueua mai piouuto, onde con ragione si poteua dire, ch'ella hauesse con la sua venuta illustrata la Città, come era scritto nella porta dalla banda verso la Città nel modo, che ho detto di sopra, cioè. *Vrbem aduentus tui lumine illustratam*. Et poi tutti li giorni mentre S. M. stette in Ferrara continuò il buon tempo, doue prima era stato per il più tempo cattiuo : Talmente che con la sua venuta la Regina non solo rallegrò tutta la Città in maniera, che ciaschduno giubilaua d'allegrezza, vedendo vna così bella, diuota, santa, & Grandissima Regina, ma anco portò seco il buon tempo: Passata che fù la porta furono sparati molti pezzi di artiglieria in segno di allegrezza,& andò la caualcata per la via delli Angioli, che è vna lunga, bella, & diritta strada con l'ordine infratcritto.

Prima andorno molti cariaggi, liquali come hò detto di sopra, cominciorno a passare fino dalla mattina à bon'hora, poi vna squadra di archibugieri à cauallo di Sua M. & dietro a quelli vna compagnia di cauallieri con lancie, & con banderole negre, & sue trombette auanti. Dopoi vna compagnia di archibugieri à cauallo del Papa, con vna compagnia di lancie del Monaldesco con le loro trombe, dopoi le valigie de'Cardinali, & dopo loro vn Trombetto della Regina, dietro al quale veniua vna lunga caualcata de Gentil'huomini, & Cortegiani della Regina, & Arciduca, mesticati con curiali, & cortegiani de' Cardinali, che durò vn pezzo à passare, & trà questi ancora passorno due bellissime carozze della Regina, cioè quella di velluto rosso, che l'haueua donato

nato il Papa nella quale S. M. come hò detto, era venuta fino al cafone, & vn'altra di broccato d'oro riccio, fopra riccio, bellifsima, & ricchifsima con fei caualli, & doi cocchieri della medefima liurea, & poi vna lettica di S. M. appreffo del medefimo broccato come quello della carozza. Dopo caualcorno noue Trombetti della Regina, tutti veftiti di nero con le banderole delle trombe nere, & armi della Regina, & auanti di loro caualcaua vno che fonaua doi tamburri alla vfanza moreica. Et dietro a quefti feguitaua vna buona, & lunga caualcata di Gentil'huomini nobili, & Baroni, & Signori Titolati, tanto della Regina, Arciducheffa, & Arciduca, come altri forattieri di diuerfi luoghi della Lombardia, & anco de'Ferrarefi. Tra quefti non vennero nè il Duca di Seffa, nè meno il Conteftabile, liquale con alcuni altri Signori Grandi di Spagna, fubito che la Regina fi congiunfe co'l Sacro Collegio, fi fpinfero innanzi, & poi afpettorno la Regina, nella fcala auanti al Salone grande del Conciftoro publico.

Dietro alli Baroni caualcorno li Mazzieri dell'Illuftrifsimi Signori Cardinali, & poi doi Mazzieri del Papa, trà liquali caualcorno, M. Paolo Alaleone, & M. Guido Peroffo, Maeftro de ceremonia, & dietro di loro l'illuftriff. & Reuerendifsimi Signori Cardinali, a doi, à doi, cominciando dai più vecchi, & nell'vltimo loco, caualcò la Regina, trà li doi primi Diaconi, cioè Sforza, & Mont'alto, & dietro a lei l'Arciducheffa Madre, & l'Arciduca Alberto, & poi la Ducheffa di Gandia Cameriera Maggiore di S. M. & alcune delle Dame più principali in carrozza, & dietro a quelle li Prelati afsiftenti nelle mule Pontificali, & dalle bande cominciando dalli primi Cardinali, andauano li Sguzzeri della guardia di S. S. & all'vltimo per retroguardia veniua vna fquadra di Arcieri dell' Arciduca, che faceuano bellifsima vifta, & poi li caualli leggieri di Sua Santità.

Arriuati che furono al Palazzo, entrorno tutti fotto all'arco predetto auanti la piazza, & Chiefa Cathedrale, & li Signori Cardinali fubito fmontati, andorno alla ftanza de'paramenti, che era vna camera contigua a detto falone, & à man manca dell'Ingreffo. Et perche l'illuftriff. & Reuerendiff. Cardinali, Sforza, & Mont'alto, primo Diacono haueuano da feruire al Papa in veftirlo de'Sacri paramenti, la Regina reftò in mezo trà l'Illuftriff. & Reuerendifsimi Cardinali, Farnefe, & Santi Quattro, liquali l'accompagnorno alle ftanze dell'Illuftriff. Signore Cardinale Aldobrandino vicino a detto falone, a man finiftra della loggia, che vi ftà auanti, nelle quali ftanze S. M. fi trattenne fin tanto che fu tempo di effer introdotta in Conciftoro publico. Et trà tanto fu parato il Papa di anutto, camifo, fiola, Piniale roffo, & Mitra pretiofa, & precedendo la Croce fe ne venne in Conciftoro, che già era l'Auemaria, & per quello furono appicciate tutte le fopradette torciere, con molte altre torcie, che tennero li Palafrenieri, & Scudieri di Sua Santità, accioche il falone foffe bene illuminato. All'hora li Cantori cominciorno à far vna bella, & fuaue mufica, che durò mentre li Cardinali, preftorno l'obedienza quale finita che fu, & effendo già partiti li doi primi Diaconi, per andare a pigliare la Regina ceffò la mufica, & il Signore Bernardino Scotto, auuocato Conciftoriale

riale cominciò a proporre la fua caufa, con vn proemio elegante, nel quale efpofe la grandezza di quefta Regina, che veniua comparandola alla Regina Sabba, che dall'eftreme parti del mondo, andò à trouar Salomone, & auanti che hauefse finito il proemio, entrorno in Conciftoro l'Illuftrifs. & Reuerendifsimi Signori Cardinali Farnefe, & Santi Quattro. Onde l'Auuocato fu coftretto a tacere fin tanto, che detti Cardinali andorno all'obedienza, & dopoi feguitò la fua caufa abbreuiando, & venendo prefto al fine, per che già fi fentiua, che la Regina era arriuata alla porta del Salone condotta dalli doi predetti primi Diaconi, cioè Sforza, & Mont'alto, auanti a i quali andauano M. Paolo, & M. Guido Maftri di ceremonie,& il Signor Ciouan Francefco Aldobrandino per moftrare a Sua M. quando fi haueua da ingenocchiare;& dietro la Regina veniuano immediatamente l'Arciduchefsa Madre, & l'Arciduca Alberto, & poi molte Dàme principali di S. M. laquale arriuata,che fu nel principio della quadratura d' banchi de' Cardinali, efsendofi riftretti tutti di quà, & di là,& lafciata la via di mezo ftrigata in maniera che la Regina potefse veder S. Santità fe inginocchiò la prima volta con vna gratia, & maeftà mirabile, & dipoi la feconda nel mezo della quadratura,& la terza nel piano del Solio,doue inginocchiata bafciò il piede prima, & poi la mano di S.Santità.che con grande allegrezza,& tenerezza di cuore la riceuè. Subito dopò della Regina immediatamente bafciò il piede, & la mano al Papa,l'Arciduchefsa Madre, & dopò lei l'Arciduca Alberto, quale dopò hauer bafciato il piede, & la mano fu da Sua Santità abbraciato con fingolare amoreuolezza. Et per non far ftar la Regina in piedi a difaggio,fenza che nfsun'altro per all'hora bafciafse il piede a S. Santità, fe ben molti lo defierauano, & fpetialmente le Dame della Regina,fu finito il Conciftoro, & S. Santità con i Cardinali fè ne tornò alla predetta ftanza de paramenti, ma prima commandò à quattro de più antichi Cardinali Diaconi, che furono li Illuftrifsimi, & Reuerendifsimi Sforza, Mont'alto, Farnefe, & Santi Quattro, che infieme con l'Illuftrifsimo Cardinale Aldobrandino,accompagnafsero la Regina alle fue ftanze,& all'hora li Mufici di nuouo cominciorno à cantare, & durò la mufica fin tanto che la Regina fu vfcita dalla fala quale fu poi guidata, & accompagnata da detti Signori Cardinali fino alle fue ftanze conducendola per vn corridore a man dritta della fopradetta fala, & fu lafciata da detti Signori Cardinali, nella fua anticamera infieme con l'Arciduchefsa Madre, & l'Arciduca, & poco dopò che furono partiti li Cardinali la Regina con la Madre fi ritirò nella fua camera vltima, & l'Arciduca fu accompagnato dall'Illuftrifs. Signor Giouan Francefco Aldobrandino alle ftanze afsegnateli,che come hò detto di fopra,fono quelle doue foleua ftare il Signore Cardinale Aldobrandino.

Il giorno feguente, che fu fabbato alli 14. la Regina con la Madre,& Arciduca dopò hauer vdito due Mefse, come fogliono fare ogni giorno vna per li morti, & l'altra per li viui, furono inuitate a pranfo da Sua Santità, che li diede da mangiare nella fua anticamera, doue furono apparecchiate doi, ò per dir meglio tre tauole vna per S. Santità, & vn palmo da quella lontana vn'altra per la Regina, quafi della medefima altezza, & vn'altra a quella congiunta in ta in maniera, che non vi si vedeua differenza, & parena tutta vna tauola per l'Arciducheſſa, & Arciduca. Sedè la Regina in vn ſcabello con poſtergale coperto di velluto cremeſino, & l'Arciducheſſa, & Arciduca in doi ſcabelli ſemplici con appoggi ſimili à quelli, che ſogliono ſeruire per il Conciſtoro ſe-creto, & tutti federono da vna banda per il medeſimo verſo, che fedeua il Papa, il quale era ſeruito dal ſuo Scalco, Coppieri, Trinciante, & Miniſtri ſoliti, con ſeruitio, & piatto particolare, & la Regina con l'altre due Altez-ze fu ſeruita da vn'altro Scalco, che fu il Sig. Saſſatello con trinciante partico-lare, & altri miniſtri neceſſarij tutti ſeruitori di S. Santità, eccetto li coppie-ri, che cia ſcheduna delle ſopradette Altezze haueua il ſuo particolare, & la Regina oltre il coppiere era ſeruita dal Duca di Gandia, che li leuaua, & met-teua il piatto inanzi, & dal Duca di Seſia, che quando beueua le porgeua la ſaluietta, & il Conteſtabile la ſeruì di coppa, quale portaua in mano ſenza ſottocoppa, ma coperta con vn coperchio di criſtallo, & ogni volta prima che beueſſe la Regina votaua vn poco di vino nel coperchio, & li faceua la credenza, il che non fu oſſeruato da gli altri coppieri della Madre, & Arci-duca à quali ſi daua à bere in bichieri ſenza coperchio, & non ſe gli faceua credenza alcuna, che ſi vedeſſe.

Il Papa quando voleua dire alcuna coſa alla Regina ſi ſeruiua del Signor Franceſco di Atriſtani ſuo Cameriero nobile Thedeſco, & Cameriere di Sua Santità, il quale ſeruiua per interprete tra il Papa, & S. Maeſtà.

Domenica li 15. di Nouembre fu fatto il ſolenne ſpoſalitio, & l'altare fu adornato con ſette candelieri grandi d'argento indorati, con ſette candele ſimilmente indorati, & con vna belliſſima Croce di criſtallo di montagna, & dento ve n'è vn groſſo pezzo di quella ſopra la quale N. S. Gieſu Chriſto per dar ſalute à noi volſe morire, & vi furono ancora poſte tutte /ſe ſtatue di ar-gento delli 12. Apoſtoli, & fu parato con doi palij belliſſimi di color roſſo dall'vna, & l'altra parte dell'altare; & in mezo auanti alla Croce vi fu poſta la roſa d'oro, che S. Santità la quarta Domenica della Quareſima proſsima paſſata benediſſe, quale donò poi nel fin della Meſſa alla Regina come appreſ-ſo ſi dirà. Dietro all'altare nel piano del ſopradetto tauolato furono fatti doi palchetti, vno con tre ſcalini baſsi, il cui piano era quadro, & largo per ogni verſo ſette piedi poſto dalla banda deſtra dell'altare, & appoggiato al muro, ſopra il quale ſta il pulpito doue ſogliono ſtare i Cantori ordinarij della Chie-ſa, che viene ad eſſere à punto ſcontro all'organo; ſopra il qual pulpito non vi andò quel giorno ne cantori, ne altra perſona. Fu detto palchetto coperto tutto per terra di panni roſsi, & ſopra vi fù tirata vna cortina a foggia della buſſola, che ſtà inanzi alla camera del Papa della medeſima grandezza, che era il palco, & fatta di nuouo del medeſimo broccato, & tela di argento come erano li paramenti della camera di S. Maeſtà, & le cortine ſi poteuauo aprire dalla banda dinanzi; & vi furono poſte due ſedie baſſe di broccato, vna per la Regina à man diritta, & vna per l'Arciducheſſa ſua Madre à man manca, con doi coſcini della medeſima tela di argento dinanzi per poteruiſi ingenocchia-re. Et dall'altra banda ſotto all'organo fu fatto vn'altro palchetto della

mede-

medefima grandezza, ma con doi foli fcalini, & con cortine di damafco roffo nella medefima forma, come erano quelle della Regina con vna fedia per l'Arciduca, doue haueuano da ftare à fentire la Meffa.

Verfo le fedici hore S. Santità partendofi dal Caftello à cauallo venne alla Chiefa, doue già erano congregati tutti li Cardinali parati di paramenti rofsi ciafcheduno conforme all'ordine fuo in vna cappella, & luogo preparato à man dritta dell'ingreffo della Chiefa, & vicino alla porta, & mentre S. Santità fi paraua in detto luogo, arriuò in Chiefa la Regina accompagnata da doi Cardinali Diaconi, che furono Farnefe, & Santiquattro, infieme con l'Arciducheffa Madre, & l'Arciduca Alberto, & molti Sign. grandi, & nobili Baroni di Spagna, & da forfe 22. dame, & Sign. Principali. Et comparfe S. Maeftà quella mattina non in habito di lutto come era comparfa il giorno della entrata, ma con vna ricchifsima vefte di tela di argento ricamata, & adorna di molte gioie, & tutte le fue Dame erano nobilifsimamente veftite con habiti fuperbifsimi, & gioie infinite. Così anco l'Arciduca comparue eftito di bianco con vna cappa di velluto guarnita cô trine, & ricami d'oro bellifsimi, & dietro al capuccio vi erano 36. diamanti belli, & grandi, che valeuano vn theforo, & nella rofa della berretta oltre molte altre perle, & gioie vi era vn diamante grande quanto vna onghia del dito groffo. Così anco il Duca di Seffa, il Conteftabile, & tutti li Grandi, & Baroni titolati comparuero veftiti fuperbifsimamente con adorni di oro, & argento, & gioie infinite, & la guardia delli Tedefchi di S. Maeftà comparue non veftita di nero, ma con habito di velluto cremefino, & tafetano giallo, & alabarde tutte indorate come fogliono vfare li Sguizzeri delle guardie fenza cappa, ò mantello, & quelli dell' Arciduca erano veftiti di velluto nero, così anco li Cauallegieri di S. Maeftà mutorno le banderole, & comparuero con cafache di velluto cremefino, & ogni cofa apparue piena di fplendore, & allegrezza, & fi viddero infinite ricchifsime, & belle liuree di detti Grandi, Baroni, & Sign. Titolati, che hora non poffo, ne sò meglio riferire. Paffata, che fu la Regina, & arriuata al fuo palco, al quale fi afcendeua per diece fcalini, che erano cuftoditi dalla guardia de fuoi Tedefchi, andò S. Maeftà à federe nel detto luogo per lei preparato infieme con l'Arciducheffa fua Madre, & l'Arciduca Alberto andò fimilmente à federe al fuo luogo fopradetto, & le Dame della Regina fi accomodorno nel piano del palco à canto, & intorno alla cortina di S. Maeftà, appreffo la quale era pofto vn banco fenza poftergale, fopra il quale federono cinque Grandi di Spagna, cioè il Duca di Seffa, il Conteftabile, il Duca di Gandia, il Duca di Vmala, & il Prencipe di Oranges. Tutti gli altri Signori, & Baroni Titolati flettero in piedi. Appreffo dell'Arciduca fuori della cortina in vno fcabello fedè il Conte di Borlemon Caualier del Tofone, & come alcuni mi differo Gran Marefcial di Fiandra, & in piedi à canto la detta cortina ftaua vn Cameriero, ò vero Maftro di camera di S. A. veftito di habito clericale, & à canto al muro quafi fcontro al talamo della Regina ftauano tre Signori nobili, che teneuano in mano ciafcheduno vn baftone, & mi fu detto, che quefti erano li Maiordomi della Regina; dell'Arciducheffa, & dell'Arciduca.

duca. Fù anco deputato Monf. Visconte Suddiacono Apostolico, che steste
sempre appresso la cortina della Regina per mostrarli quando S. Maestà si haueua da leuare in piede, ò sedere, ò inginocchiarsi.

Trattanto S. Santità ancora essendo già parata di amitto, camiso, cingu-
lo, stola, piuiale rosso, & Regno pretioso cioè il Clementino fatto di nouo da
S. Santità bellissimo, & ricchissimo di gioie, quanto si sia quello di Papa Giulio secondo, precedendo li Cubicularij, & Camerieri di S. Santità con veste
rosse, & capucci, & li Capellani, che portauano tutti li altri Regni, & Mitre
pretiose di S. Santità, & poi gli Auditori di Rota, Maestro del Sacro Palazzo,
Suddiaconi Apostolici, & vn Accolito co'l turribulo, & nauicella, & dietro di
lui sette altri, tra Accoliti, & Abbreuiatori, che portauano sette candelieri
con sette candele indorate accese, & dietro di loro il Suddiacono parato con
la Croce, & appresso di lui li Vescoui parati con piuiale, & mitra, & poi li
Cardinali similmente parati, secondo l'ordine loro à doi, à doi, S. Santità
montò in sedia, & sotto il baldachino se ne venne verso la cappella, & si fermò prima à fare oratione auanti l'altare del Santissimo Sacramento, & dipoi
arriuato auanti l'altare maggiore, & fatta iui ancora vn poco di oratione, se
ne andò alla sedia de' paramenti, che staua nel corno sinistro dell'altare, doue
tutti li Cardinali prima, che furono diecinoue, & l'istessi, che ho nominati di
sopra, & poi tutti li Vescoui parati, che furono 28. andorno à render l'obedienza secondo il solito à S. Santità la quale dopo leuatasi in piedi, & deposta
la mitra, cominciò l'hora di terza, & mentre si cantaua il primo salmo da i
cantori pigliò i sandali, & le scarpe leggendo in tanto S. Santità li salmi, &
orationi preparatorie per la messa, & nel fine di terza cantò l'oratione secondo il solito, & poi se lauò le mani la prima volta, seruendolo in portar l'acqua
l'Ambasciatore di Bologna, & lauato che si hebbe le mani depose la mitra, il
piuiale, stola, & cingolo, & dalli doi Cardinali Diaconi assistenti, che furono
Sforza, & Montalto, insieme col Cardinal di Cesis, che haueua da cantar
l'Euangelio, & M. Matteo Benzi Suddiacono Apostolico fu parato di tutti li
paramenti pontificali per la Messa, cioè del cingolo col suo succintorio, della
Croce pettorale, del fanone, della stola, della tunicella, della dalmatica, de i
guanti, della pianeta, del pallio con le sue spille, & dell'anello quale gli pose
il Cardinale di Fiorenza, che serui S. Santità in luogo di Vescouo Cardinale
assistente, de' quali in Ferrara non ve n'era alcuno, & vsò il piuiale, ma senza
formale, & finalmente S. Santità prese la mitra pretiosa, & posto prima l'in-
censo nel turribulo processionalmente discese dalla detta sedia, & andò verso
l'altare per celebrar la Messa, & nel mezo della quadratura auanti l'altare fu
incontrato dalli tre vltimi preti Cardinali, che furono Auila, Gueuara, &
Arigoni, li quali l'abbracciorno, & basciorno sopra l'homero sinistro, secondo
il solito, dopoi fu cominciata, & seguitata la Messa con tutte le ceremonie solite, & descritte nel libro ceremoniale, quando il Papa celebra personalmen-
te, & la Messa fu de Spirito Santo, & per questo S. Santità prima, che si cantasse
l'Euangelio discese dal Solio, & se inginocchiò nel faldistorio al Versiculo.
Veni Creator Spiritus.

Cantato

Cantato che fu il Credo da i cantori, & letto dal Papa che all'hora ſtaua nel Solio Pontificale l'offertorio prima che ſi lauaſſe le mani la ſeconda volta, l'Illuſtriſsimi & Reuerendiſsimi Signori Cardinali Farneſe, & Santi Quattro andorno al talamo della Regina, & con le debite riuerenze la conduſſero nel Solio, à i piedi di Sua Santità, & ſeco dopò lei venne l'Arciducheſſa Madre, & l'Arciduca Alberto con tutti li predetti Grandi di Spagna, & le Dame di S. Maeſtà, quali aſpettorno à baſſo à piedi al Solio nel piano della cappella. Et ſtando la Regina, & Arciducheſſa in piedi auanti S. Santità, fu letto da Monſignor Barberino Protonotario Apoſtolico il mandato della procura della Maeſtà del Rè Filippo, fatto in perſona del Sereniſsimo Alberto Arciduca di Auſtria, acciò che in nome ſuo poteſſe ſpoſare detta Regina, la quale finito che fù di leggere il mandato s'inginocchiò à man manca dell'Arciduca ſopra doi coſcini di tela di argento, & l'Arciduca ſopra doi altri di velluto roſſo; & all'hora il Papa ſedendo con la Mitra diſſe le parole ſoſtantiali del matrimonio, interrogando l'vno, & l'altro nella ſeguente forma, cioè prima l'Arciduca, & dicendo queſte preciſe parole.

Dilecte Fili Alberte Archidux Auſtriæ, vis tu tamquam procurator cariſſimi in Chriſto filij noſtri Philippi Hiſpaniarum Regis Catholici, & eius nomine deſponſare, & pro eo ducere in vxorem dilectiſſimam in Chriſto filiam noſtram Margaritam Archiduciſſam Auſtriæ hic præſentem, & promittis quod dictus cariſſimus in Chriſto filius noſter Philippus Rex illam tamquam ſuam legitimam ſponſam, & vxorem tenebit, & tractabit ſecundum id quod diſponit, & mandat Sacroſancta Romana, & Apoſtolica Eccleſia?

Et l'Arciduca riſpoſe *Volo, & ita promitto.*
Dopoi S. Santità interrogò la Regina, dicendo.

Dilectiſſima in Chriſto filia noſtra Margarita Archiduciſſa Auſtriæ vis cariſſimum in Chriſto filium noſtrum Philippum Hiſpaniarum Regem Catholicum abſentem in tuum legitimum ſponſum, & maritum, & eius nomine deſponſari à dilecto filio noſtro Alberto Archiduce Auſtriæ hic præſente, & promittis tenere, & tractare d. Cariſſimum in Chriſto filium noſtrum Philippum Regem pro tuo legitimo ſponſo, & marito ſecundum id quod diſponit, & mandat Sacroſancta Romana, & Apoſtolica Eccleſia?

Quali parole acciò che meglio fuſſero inteſe dalla Regina furono interpretate de verbo ad verbum, & lette in lingua Tedeſca dal Signor Franceſco di Atriſtani Cameriero ſecreto di S. Santità, & la Regina hauendole bene inteſe prima che reſpondeſſe con vna gratia mirabile ſi voltò verſo la

Madre

Madre quaſi domandandole licenza, ſe ſi contentaua che preſtaſſe il conſenſo al detto matrimonio, & hauuto da lei l'aſſenſo riſpoſe in lingua Tedeſca, che ſi contentaua dicendo, come poi interpretò il ſopradetto Signor Franceſco *Volo, & ita promitto.*

Trattanto il Suddiacono Apoſtolico che haueua cantata la Epiſtola Latina preſo dall'altare l'anello lo portò ſopra vna coppa d'oro coperta con vn velo, & poſtoſi inginocchione auanti S. Santità, aſpettò finche S. Beatitudine leuatoſi in piedi, & depoſta la mitra lo benediſſe con li ſeguenti verſicoli, & orationi, cioè.

℣. *Adiutorium noſtrum in nomine Domini.*
℞. *Qui fecit cœlum, & terram.*

Oremus.
Benedic Domine hunc anulum fidei coniugalis ſignum quem in nomine Domini noſtri Ieſu Chriſti benedicimus † vt qui eo coniuncti deſignantur in tua pace conſiſtant, & in tua voluntate permaneant, & in tuo amore viuant, & ſeneſcant, & multiplicentur in longitudine dierum. Per eund. Chriſtum dominum noſtrum.

Oremus.
Creator, & conſeruator humani generis, dator gratiæ ſpiritualis, largitor æternæ ſalutis, tu Domine ſpiritum ſanctum tuum paracletum de cœlis ſuper hunc anulum emitte, vt qui eum tradiderit, & qui eum geſtauerit ſint armati virtute cœleſtis defenſionis, & proficiat illis ad æternam ſalutem per Dominum noſtrum, qui tecum viuit, & regnat in vnitate eiuſdem Spiritus Sancti Deus per omnia ſæcula ſæculorum. ℞. Amen.

Et finite le dette orationi preſo l'aſperſorio di mano del Cardinale di Aſcoli primo prete di quelli che ſedeuano nel banco de' Cardinali, che à queſto effetto fu chiamato, aſperſe l'anello con l'acqua benedetta; Dopoi ſedendo con la mitra S. Santità pigliò detto anello, & lo conſegnò all'Arciduca, il qual lo miſe nel dito annulare della man deſtra della Regina, dicendo tra tanto il Papa le ſeguenti parole, cioè.

Anulo ſuo ſubarret te Dominus Jeſus Chriſtus, & tamquam ſponſam decoret te corona.

Et li Cantori riſpoſero *Amen.* Et coſi ſempre riſpoſero alli Verſicoli, quando fù biſogno.

Dopoi S. Santità leuataſi in piedi, & depoſta la mitra benediſſe li ſpoſi dicendo li ſeguenti verſicoli, benedittioni, ſalmi, & orationi, cioè.

℣. *Benedicti ſitis à Domino.*
℞. *Qui mundum ex nihilo fecit*
℣. *Adiutorium noſtrum in nomine Domini.*
℞. *Qui fecit cœlum, & terram.*

Benedicat vos Deus Pater † cuſtodiat vos Dei filius, † Illuminet vos Spiritus Sanctus Oſtendat Dominus vultum ſuum vobis, & miſereatur veſtri, Conuertat Dominus faciem ſuam ſuper vos, & det vobis pacem omnibus diebus vitæ veſtræ, impleatque uos Dominus omni benedictione cœleſti † in remiſſionem omnium peccatorum veſtrorum Amen.

C   *Mandet*

℣. Mandet Deus virtute suæ.

℞. Confirma hoc Deus quod operatus es in nobis.

℣. A templo sancto tuo quod est in Hierusalem.

℞. Tibi offerent Reges munera.

℣. Domine exaudi orationem meam.

℞. Et clamor meus ad te veniat.

℣. Dominus vobiscum.

℞. Et cum spiritu tuo.

Oremus.

Omnipotens, & misericors Deus, qui primos parentes nostros Adam, & Euam sua virtu te copulauit, ipse corpora vestra sanctificet, & benedicat † atque in societate, & amore veræ dilectionis coniungat. per Dom. nostrum. ℞. Amen.

Oremus.

Deus Abraam, Deus Isac, Deus Iacob benedic famulum tuum Philippum Regem, & hanc ancillam tuam Margaritam Reginam eius Sponsam, & semina semen uitæ æternæ in mentibus eorum, vt quicquid pro vtilitate didicerint hoc facere cupiant. Per Christum dom. nostrum. ℞. Amen.

Dopoi il Papa sedendo senza mitra, ma col berettino lesse il salmo 127. cioè Beati omnes qui timent dominum, &c. quale i cantori cantorno in musica, & finito che fù, S. Santità di nuouo leuatosi in piede, disse li seguenti versicoli, & orationi, cioè.

Kirie eleison. Christe eleison. Kirie eleison. Pater noster.

℣. Et ne nos inducas in tentationem

℞. Sed libera nos à malo.

℣. Saluum fac seruum tuum, & ancillam tuam.

℞. Deus meus sperantes in te.

℣. Mitte eis domine auxilium di Sancto

℞. Et de syon tuere eos

℣. Esto eis Domine turis fortitudinis,

℞. A facie inimici.

℣. Domine exaudi orationem meam.

℞. Et clamor meus ad te veniat.

℣. Dominus vobiscum

℞. Et cum spiritu tuo.

Oremus.

Deus qui tam excellenti mysterio coniugalem copulam consecrasti ut Christi, & Ecclesiæ sacramenta præsignares in fœdere nuptiarum, presta quesumus, vt quod nostro ministratur officio tua benedictione impleatur, Per Christum Dom. nostrum. ℞. Amen.

Oremus.

Propitiari Domine supplicationibus nostris, & institutis tuis quibus propagationem humani generis ordinasti benignus assiste, vt quod te auctore iungitur, te auxiliante seructur. Per Christ. dom. nostrum. ℞. Amen.

Oremus.

Deus qui potestate virtutis tuæ de nibilo cuncta fecisti quique dispositis vniuersitatis exordijs

exordijs, *homini ad imaginem Dei fatto,ideo Inseparabile mulieris adiutorium condidisti*, *vt foemineo corpore de virili dares carni principium,docens quod semel placuisset introiti nunquam liceret disiungi,Benedic quesumus hanc coniunctionem, & sicut misisti Angelum tuum adTobiam,& Saram filiam Raguelis,ita digneris domine mittere benedictionem tuam super famulum tuum Philippum Regem,& hanc Ancillam tuam Margaritam Reginam, eius sponsam, vt in tua semper voluntate permaneant,& in tuo amore viuant, & senescant, & multiplicentur in longitudine dierum.Per Christum Dominum nostrum. R. Amen.*

Oremus.

Deus per quem mulier iungitur viro,& societas principalis ordinata ea benedictione donatur, quæ nec sola per originalis peccati pœnam,nec per diluuij est ablata sententiam,respice propitius super hanc famulam tuam Margaritam Reginam quæ maritali iungenda con sortio tua se expetit protectione muniri;sit in ea iugum dilectionis, & pacis,fidelis , & casta nubat in Christo,imitatrixque Sanctarum permaneat fæminarum , sit amabilis vt Rachaël viro suo,sapiens vt Rebecca,longeua & fidelis vt Sara nihil in ea ex actibus suis ille auctor præuaricationis vsurpet Nixa fidei mandatis permaneat vni thoro iuncta, Contactus illicitos fugiat,muniat infirmitatem suam robore disciplinæ,sit verecundia grauis,sit pudore venerabilis,sit doctrinis cœlestibus erudita,sit fæcunda in sobole, sit probata , & innocens,& ad beatorum requiem,atque ad cælestia regna perueniat, & videat filios filiorum suorum vsque ad tertiam , & quartam generationem , & ad optatam perueniat senectutem . Per Christum Dominum Nostrum. R. Amen.

Dipoi dise il Papa.

Benedictio Dei patris omnipotentis, & Filij; & Spiritus Sancti descendat super Charissimo in Christo filium nostrum Philippum Hispaniarum Regem Catholicum ; & Carissimam hanc in Christo Filiam nostram Margaritam Reginam eius vxorem. R. Amen.

Et poi soggionse.

Quos Deus Coniunxit homo non separet.

Et mentre dicea queste parole,pigliò la mano destra dell'Arciduca,& la po se sopra la mano destra della Regina seguitando di dire . *Ita vos ego coniungo in nomine Patris,*† *& Filij,* †*& Spiritus Sancti* † *Amen.*

Et finalmente pigliando l'aspersorio li asperse con l'acqua Santa, & disse alla Regina , *Vostra Maestà vada in pace* . Et subito ella inginocchione come staua baciò il piede prima , & poi la mano a Sua Santità per il fauore che gli haueua fatto, & fatica che haueua per lei durata, & poi fu condotta dalli medesimi doi Cardinali Diaconi al suo Talamo, accompagnata dall'Arciduchessa Madre, & dalle sue Dame, & Grandi di Spagna .

Ma l'Arciduca Alberto restò nel Solio, per il secondo matrimonio, per il quale fu chiamato il Signor Duca di Sessa, procuratore della Sereniísima Infante , & Monsignor Barberino lesse il mandato di procura , & Sua Santità fece l'interrogationi,benedisse li anelli , & poi li sposi con tutti li versiculi, Psalmi, & Orationi poste di sopra, mutato solamente il nome doue bisognaua, & l'interrogationi furono di questa maniera .

Dilecte

Dilecte fili Alberte Archidux Austriæ, vis dilectissimàm in Christo filiam nostram Isabellam Hispaniarum Infantem absentem in tuam legitimam sponsam, & vxorem, & eius nomine, & vti eius procuratorem desponsare dilectum filium nostrum Antonium Ducem Sessæ hic præsentem, & promittis d. dilectissimam filiam nostram Isabellam tenere, & tractare pro tua legitima sponsa, & vxore secundum id, quod disponit Sacro Sancta Romana, & Apostolica Ecclesia?

Et l'Arciduca rispose. *Volo, & ita promitto.*

Dopò il Papa interrogò il Duca di Sessa, in questa forma. *Dilecte fili Antoni Dux Sessæ vis tu tamquam procurator dilectissimæ in Christo filiæ nostræ Isabellæ Hispaniarum Infantis, & eius nomine accipere anulum, & desponsari à dilecto filio nostro Alberto Archiducæ Austriæ hic præsente, & promittis, quod dicta dilecta filia nostra Isabella illum tractabit, & tenebit tamquam suum legitimum sponsum, & maritum secundum id quod disponit, & mandat Sacrosancta Romana, & Apostolica Ecclesia?*

Et il Duca rispose. *Volo, & ita promitto.*

Et quando l'Arciduca messe l'anello al Duca di Sessa in nóme dell'Infante il Papa disse.

Anulo suo subarret Dominus noster Jesus Christus, dilectissimam in Christo filiam nostram Isabellam Hispaniarum Infantem, & tamquam sponsam decoret, eam corona. ℞. Amen.

Et nel fine quando il Papa li dette la benedittione, disse.

Benedictio Dei Patris omnipotentis, & Filij, & Spiritus sancti, descendat super hunc dilectum filium nostrum Albertum Archiducem, & dilectissimam in Christo filiam nostram Isabellam Hispaniarum Infantem eius vxorem. ℞. Amen.

Finita la benedittione del secondo matrimonio l'Arciduca bascià il piede, la mano, & la faccia di Sua Beatitudine, quale tanto a nome della Maestà del Rè Filippo, come anco a nome proprio con humili, & cortesi parole, ringratiò per la fatica, che S. Santità si era presa in farli tanto singolarissimo fauore, & poi si partì, & tornò al suo luogo.

Et all'hora il Signor Giouan Francesco Aldobrandino, portò li bacili per lauare le mani a Sua Santità, la seconda volta, quale lauate S. Beatitudine discese dal Solio, & andò all'Altare, doue offerì l'Hostia, & il Calice, incensò l'Altare, & fu incensato, & si lauò le mani la terza volta, portandoli l'acqua l'Am

basciatore

baſciatore di Venetia, & poi ſeguitò la Meſſa con le ſolite ceremonie.

All'offertorio dopò che furono incenſati, il Papa, & li Cardinali aſsiſtenti mentre il Cardinal Diacono cominciò ad incenſare li Cardinali preti, Monſignor Anſaldo Doſſat Veſcouo di Rodone, vno delli Prelati aſsiſtenti di S. Santità parato con piuiale, con vn'altro turribulo andò al Talamo della Regina, quale all'hora ſtaua inginocchiata, & io gli accennai che ſi leuaſſe in piede, come fece, & detto Veſcouo l'incensò due volte dopoi laſciò il Turribulo in mano di M. Adorno Suddiacono Apoſtolico, il qual incensò prima l'Arciducheſſa, ſimilmente con due incenſature, e poi l'Arciduca nel medeſimo modo.

La pace poi al ſuo tempo fu portata alla Regina con l'inſtrumento dal Suddiacono Apoſtolico, che haueua cantata l'Epiſtola latina, & coſi anco dal medeſimo fu data all'Arciducheſſa, & l'Arciduca, ma a i Cardinali la diede il Cardinal di Fiorenza aſsiſtenti, cioè alli capi di ordine ſecondo il ſolito, & poi al primo Veſcouo aſsiſtenti di Sua Santità.

Dopò che ſi furono communicati dal Papa, il Diacono Cardinale, che haueua cantato l'Euangelio, & il Suddiacono latino ſecondo il ſolito, detto Cardinal Diacono cantò il Confiteor per la communione della Regina, Arciducheſſa, Arciduca, & Duca di Seſſa, & cantato che l'hebbe, ſe ne tornò all'altare, doue preſa la piſſide con l'hoſtie conſacrate, con le ſolite ceremonie, la diede in mano del ſubdiacono, che la portò al Solio, & ſi fermò in piedi alla deſtra di S. Santità, & ſubito li doi predetti Cardinali Diaconi, Farneſe, & Santi Quattro andorno à condurre la Regina al ſolio per la communione, appreſſo laquale vennero l'Arciducheſſa Madre, & l'Arciduca, & poi il Duca di Seſſa con l'habito di San Iacomo, & ſi communicorno l'vno dopo l'altro, & la Regina dopò la communione fu guidata dalli medeſimi doi Cardinali Diaconi all'altare, doue pigliò la purificatione di mano del Cardinal de Ceſis, & poi la conduſſero al ſuo Talamo. Et l'Arciducheſſa, l'Arciduca, & Duca di Seſſa, preſero la purificatione di mano del Diacono Greco. Et trattanto fu chiamato l'Ambaſciatore dell'Imperatore per dar l'acqua alle mani a S. Santità, la quarta, & vltima volta, quale lauata che fu, ſe ne tornò all'altare, & finì la Meſſa.

Ma auanti che deſſe la benedittione, accioche Sua Santità non haueſſe di nuouo a tornare al Solio per dar la Roſa alla Regina, fu poſta auanti al mezo dell'Altare la ſua Sedia geſtatoria, ſenza le ſtanghe, nella quale ſedendo S. Santità fu chiamata la Regina, & di nuouo dalli predetti doi Cardinali Diaconi, condotta auanti S. Santità, doue ſtando inginocchiata ſopra vn cuſcino, S. Santità li donò la roſa già benedetta la quarta Domenica di Quareſima paſſata, come hò detto di ſopra. dicendo le ſolite parole, che ſtanno ſcritte nel libro ceremoniale, cioè.

Accipe roſam de manibus noſtris, qui licet immeriti locum Dei in terris tenemus; per quam deſignatur gaudium vtriuſq. Hieruſalem triumphantis ſcilicet, (†) militantis Eccleſiæ: per quam omnibus Chriſti fidelibus manifeſtatur flos ipſe ſpecioſiſſimus, qui eſt gaudium, & corona
Sanctorum

...rorum omnium. Suscipe hanc tu dilectissima filia, quæ secundum *seculum nobilis, potens, ac multa virtute prædicta, vt amplius omni vir-* *tute in Christo Domino nobiliteris tamquam rosa plantata super riuos* *aquarum multarum. Quam gratiam ex sua vberanti clementia tibi con-* *cedere dignetur, qui est trinus, & vnus in secula seculorum.* Amen. *In nomine Pattris, (†) Fitlij, (†) Spitritus sancti.* Amen.

Quale Rosa S.M. la consegnò al Signor Conte di Borlemont, Caualliero del Tosone, ilqual poi sempre la portò auanti la Regina, quando se ne tornò a casa.

Hauuta che hebbe la Regina dal Papa la Rosa, li bagiò di nuouo il piede, & la mano ringratiandolo di questo altro fauore, che gli haueua fatto, & poi fu accompagnata dalli predetti doi Cardinali Diaconi al suo luogo, & il Papa leuata la Sedia, dette la benedittione solenne al popolo, & concesse à tutti li presenti Indulgenza plenaria, quale publicò il Cardinale di Fiorenza.

Dopò Sua Santità deposto il Palio sopra l'altare, & i Cardinali lasciati i paramenti, & prese le cappe, & seguitando appresso la Croce, se ne tornorno tutti al luogo de' paramenti, & il Papa fu portato in Sedia, nel medesimo modo come era venuto, & con l'istesso Regno in testa, ma senza baldachino, & deposti che hebbe li paraméti in detto luogo, se ne tornò al Castello in lettica, quando già erano quasi 20. hore, essendo S. Santità assai stracco per la lunga fattione, & fatica che haueua durato.

La Regina poi nel medesimo modo come era venuta, fu accompagnata dalli doi predetti Cardinali Diaconi, Farnese, & Santi Quatro alle sue stanze, con la sua compagnia, & auanti di lei andaua immediatamente il Conte predetto di Borlemont, portando la Rosa in mano, & furono sparate all'hora, & anco quando fu stipulato il matrimonio molti pezzi d'artiglierie in segno di allegrezza, & la sera furono fatti molti fuochi per la Città, come anco si era fatto la sera che arriuò S. M. in Ferrara.

Non starò hora à raccontare la festa, & danze, che furono fatte l'istessa sera nel salone sopradetto doue fu fatto il Concistoro publico, nel quale comparuero più di cento gentildonne Ferrarese quasi tutte di vn simile habito immascherate con berrette, & pennacchiere bianche, che danzorno poi quasi fino à meza notte, ne meno dell'altre feste, che si sono fatte in Ferrara per allegrezza della venuta di questa Regina, delle mascare, che si sono viste per tre giorni continoui per il corso, di alcuni giochi fatti nelle fosse del castello con barche dalle donne di Commacchio riuestite à liurea di diuersi colori, che ballorno, danzorno, & corsero il palio in barca. Della rappresentatione di Iuditta, & Oloferne, che fu recitata dalli scolari de Padri Gesuiti in vna sala del Castello, perche non essendo questa profession mia, lascio ad altri la cura di raccontar queste cose. Ma dirò solo, che essendo stata inuitata la Regina il giorno della Domenica à passeggiare vn poco in carrozza per la Giudeca, che qui in Ferrara è la strada del corso, acciò fosse vista dal popolo, che la desideraua,

deraua, rifpofe, che effendofi communicata quella mattina non conueniua
attendere à cofe vane, ne volfe lafciarfi mai vedere, fe non per le Chiefe, &
lunedì mattina alli 16. del prefente andò à vifitare vna diuotifsima Chiefa
chiamata Santa Maria in Vado, doue vdì vna meffa de morti, & vide la reli-
quia di vn miracolo celebre, & infigne del fangue di N.S. Iefu Chrifto, che
427. anni fono miracolofamente mentre il facerdote celebraua fcaturì dal calice in maniera, che parue vna fontana, & arriuò fino alla volta, che ftaua
fopra l'altare, della qual volta hoggi fe ne vede ancora vn pezzo, & vi fi fcor-
gono le goccie del fangue roffo, che iui dal calice fcaturirono. Dopoi andò S.
Maeftà al monaftero delle Monache di S. Vito, doue vdì vn'altra Meffa de i
viui, cioè quella della feria corrente, & entrò dentro al monaftero, doue vdì
vna bellifsima mufica di voci, & varij inftromenti, che fonano quelle Monache con arte mirabile, & delettatione grandifsima di chi l'afcolta; & poi ancora andò à vifitare vn'altro monaftero delle Monache del Corpo di Chrifto,
doue fono fepolti tutti li Duchi, & Prencipi di cafa da Efte; & iui ancora fentì
vn buonifsimo concerto di mufica, ma fpecialmente vna di quelle monache,
che fù già Damicella della Ducheffa di Vrbino vltimamente defonta, la quale con tanta armonia, & fuauità di voci cantò fopra all'organo, che non fi
poteua fentir cofa di maggior delettatione in fimil fpecie, & la Regina à tutti
quei monafterij fece dar larga elemofina, & così anco ha fatto quafi à tutti li
poueri di Ferrara, effendo ella pijfsima, diuotifsima, & piena di mifericordia,
che Dio la benedica.

Quell'ifteffa mattina anchora mangiò la Regina con S. Santità infieme con
la Madre Arciducheffa, & con l'Arciduca, come haueua fatto il fabbato paf-
fato. Martedì alli 17. S. Maeftà dopò hauer vdito vna Meffa de' morti nella
fua priuata cappella, andò à fentire quella del Papa, & di nuouo di mano di S.
Santità fi communicò infieme con la Madre, & tutte le fue Dame, & ottenne
da S. Santità molte gratie, & Indulgenze per le corone, grani, & medaglie,
che fupplicò fuffero da S. Santità benedette, & quella mattina mangiò fimilmente con S. Beatitudine, infieme con la Madre, & Arciduca.

Mercordì mattina alli 18. effendo rifoluta la Regina di partirfi di Ferrara,
fu dato nome, che voleua vdir prima vna Meffa nella Chiefa Cathedrale, doue fu apparecchiato le cofe neceffarie per lei, fe ben non vi andò poi altra-
mente, anzi per non hauer feguito, ne compagnia, vdita, che hebbe vna Meffa
priuata nella fua cappella, infieme con l'Arciducheffa fua madre, & con l'Arciduca, & fua compagnia verfo le 15. hore fi partì di Ferrara, & poco dopoi
fi partì anchora appreffo lei l'Illuftrifsimo Sign. Cardinal Aldobrandino, che
per quáto fi dice li terrà cópagnia fino à Milano, & forfe anco fino à Genoua.

IL FINE.

In ROMA, Appreffo Nicolò Mutij. M.D.XCVIII.
Con licenza de' Superiori.

Engravings

PARS·PRAE CIPVA·COMITATVS·S.^{MI}·SACRAMENTI·ROMANO·PONTIFICI IN·ITINERE·PRAEVNTIS·

ARCVLA·S.^{MI}·SACRAMENTI·LECTICAE·INSTAR·IN·REDITV·ADVRBEM ASPORTATA·

ASTVRCO·ET·MVLÆ·AD·TANTVM·ADHIBITI·MINISTERIVM QVOVIS·INPOSTERVM·SERVITIO·EXIMVNTVR·

Scenes from the journey of the *Corpus Domini* from Rome to Ferrara, under the care of Monsignor Angelo Rocca, one day in advance of the pontiff, and from its return journey to Rome. Anonymous engravings in Rocca's *De Sacrosancto Christi Corpore* (1599). By permission of the Rare Book and Manuscript Library, Columbia University.

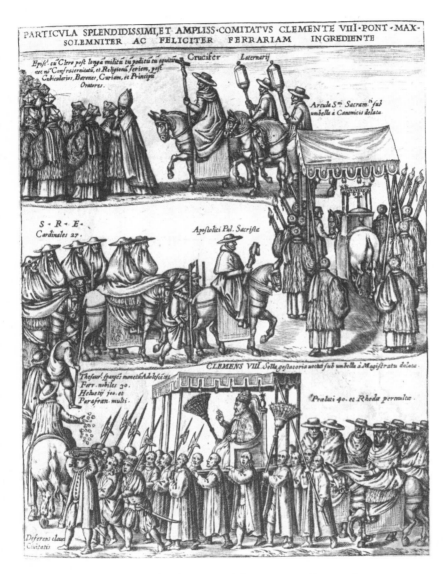

Segments of the procession for the entry of the pope into Ferrara. Anonymous engraving from Angelo Rocca's *De Sacrosancto Christi Corpore* (1599). By permission of the Rare Book and Manuscript Library, Columbia University.

Laden mules about to pass through the Porta San Giorgio, at the beginning of the long entry procession of the papal party. Both the mules and the city gate are decorated with the arms of Clement VIII. First section of a separately published engraving by Antonio Tempesta. By permission of the British Museum, Department of Prints and Drawings.

The entry of the Archduke Albert through the Porta degli Angeli, following Queen Margaret. Engraving by Jacques Callot in Giovanni Altoviti's *Essequie . . . di Margherita d'Austria* (1612), a funeral book for the queen. By permission of the Biblioteca Riccardiana-Moreniana, Florence.

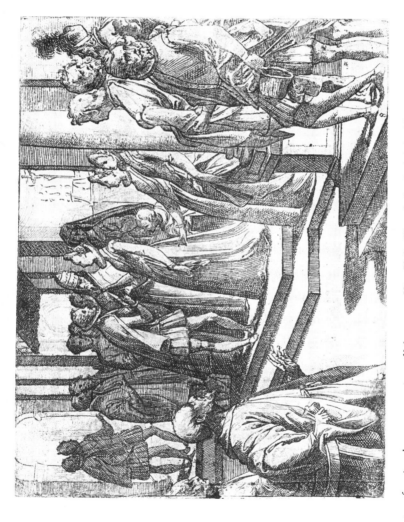

Pope Clement performing the proxy marriage of Margaret to King Philip III, with the Archduke Albert standing in for the king. Engraving by Raffaello Sciaminossi in Giovanni Altoviti's *Essequie . . . di Margherita d'Austria* (1612), a funeral book for the queen. By permission of the Biblioteca Riccardiana-Moreniana, Florence.

Indexes

Indexes

Index I refers to the Introduction, and Index II to the texts of the reproduced festival *livrets*. The first aims at including all references to persons, whether real, mythological, or allegorical, all significant references to cities, and a few abstract or general categories. Most of the general categories are for various elements present in festivals or ceremonies, namely, in alphabetical order: (1) artillery salutes, (2) *baldacchini* or ceremonial canopies, (3) banquets and other festive repasts, (4) cardinals, appearing as a body on ceremonial occasions, (5) clergy, local, appearing as a body, (6) coins, festive tossing of, (7) dancing, (8) fireworks and illuminations, (9) fountains flowing with wine, (10) inscriptions (Latin), (11) masking, (12) masses and other religious rites, (13) music and musicians, (14) orations and public prayers, (15) paintings, (16) processions, (17) sculpture, (18) theatrical productions on festive occasions, (19) triumphal arches, (20) triumphal chariots, and (21) young patricians in costume, appointed to greet and serve official guests.

The second index includes only a select number of references to persons, omitting very many mentions of people who took part in processions or ceremonies but are now wholly or nearly forgotten. Most allusions to cities are, however, included, as are also all references to churches, palaces, streets, and city gates in Ferrara. Few general categories are indexed beyond those of the various festival elements listed above.

The five reproduced *livrets* are indicated in the second index by Roman numerals, with I being the account of the departure of Cesare d'Este and entry of Cardinal Aldobrandino, II that of the entry of Pope Clement, III that recounting the entries of the Venetian ambassadors and the duke of Mantua, IV that for the entry and visit of the duke of Parma, and V that for the entry and stay of the queen of Spain.

References are to leaves, rather than to pages, with the *recto* being assumed unless a *verso* is indicated. Thus V: B2 refers to the *recto* of the second leaf of signature B in the account of the queen's entry.

Both indexes use italics to distinguish real or allegorical personages portrayed in the decorations of the *apparati*, or alluded to in the Latin inscriptions, in orations, or in public prayers. Thus, for example, there is one entry for factual or prosaic references to Pope Clement VIII and a second one, italicized, for portrayals of him in painting and sculpture, or allusions to him in inscriptions and orations.

English forms are used for names of cities, but the Italian ones are preserved for names of churches, streets, and city gates. Italian forms are kept for the names of nearly all Italian personages, including noblemen, but English forms are employed for popes and foreign sovereigns. Ruling Italian princes are listed under their Christian names, e.g., Alfonso II d'Este, but other noblemen, including those with titles, are listed under their family names, e.g., Medici, Giuliano dei, duke of Nemours. Following Italian practice, consorts retain their maiden names, often without any reference to the family names of their husbands. Thus: Este, Lucrezia d', duchess of Urbino.

The Abbreviations and Bibliography are not indexed, and there are no references to the bibliographical citations of the notes. Index I does, however, include a few references to other factual information placed in the notes. These references are to the endnote number rather than to a page.

Index I
to the Introduction

Vatican Palace, Rome, 32.
Venetian Special Ambassadors, to Duke Alfonso II, 15; to Pope Clement VIII, x, 30–31, 49, 52–53; to Queen Margaret of Spain, 38–39.
Veneto, Venetian *terra ferma*, 18, 38–39.
Venice, city and republic, 3, 4, 13, 16, 18–19, 21, 30, 31, 32, 34, 37, 38, 39, 46, 74; note 70.
Verses, recited on state occasions, 9.
Vervins, Treaty of, 1598, 29.
Vicenza, 36.
Victory, personification, 40.
Vincenzo I Gonzaga, duke of Mantua 1587–1612, xi, 31–32, 33, 34, 35, 36, 39, 43–44, 49, 52–53; note 73.
Virtue, personification, 24.
Volto del Cavallo, arch and passageway opposite the Duomo in Ferrara, 24.

Wagons, see Triumphal Chariots.
Woodcuts, 5.

Young Patricians, in costume, as participants in state pageantry, 24, 25, 28, 52.

Zwyn, river in Flanders, 46.

Index II
for the Livrets Reproduced in Facsimile

Abraham, Old Testament character, V: C1^v.
Adam, Old Testament character, V: C1^v.
Alaleone, Paolo, papal master of ceremonies, V: B2, B2^v.
Albert of Austria, 1559–1621, called the Pious, archduke, formerly cardinal, later to be co-sovereign of the southern Low Countries with his consort the Infanta Isabel, V: throughout.
Aldobrandini, Cinzio (San Giorgio in text), 1551–1610, cardinal, nephew of Pope Clement VIII, IV: A4.
Aldobrandini, Gian Francesco, captain general of the papal army, nephew of Pope Clement VIII, V: A4^v, B1, B2^v, C2^v.
Aldobrandini, Pietro, 1571–1610, cardinal, papal legate *pro latere* in Ferrara, nephew of Pope Clement VIII, I: A2^v–A4; II: A2–A2^v, A4; III: A3^v; IV: A3^v, A4; V: A1^v, A2, B1^v, B2^v, C4.
Alfonso II d'Este, duke of Ferrara 1559–1597, I: A2^v, A3^v; V: A2^v.
Ambassadors to the Holy See, appearing together on ceremonial occasions, II: A3, A4; III: A2–A2^v; IV: A3–A3^v.

Clement VIII, pope 1592–1605, I: A2, A3ᵛ; II: A1ᵛ–A4ᵛ; III: A2–A2ᵛ, A4–A4ᵛ; IV: A2, A4; V: A2, A2ᵛ, A3, A4ᵛ, B2–C3ᵛ, C4.
Clement VIII, II: A2, A4, A4ᵛ.
Clergy, Local, appearing as a body in pageantry and public ceremonies, I: A2ᵛ; II: A1ᵛ, A3, A3ᵛ, A4.
Coins, Public Tossing of, I: A3, A3ᵛ; II: A4ᵛ.
Collescipoli, locality in Umbria, II: A2.
Comacchio, town in the duchy of Ferrara, V: C3ᵛ.
Concord, I: A3ᵛ, A4.
Constable, see Fernández de Velasco, Juan.
Corpo di Cristo, convent in Ferrara.
Corpus Domini, see Host, Consecrated.
Costumes, I: A2ᵛ, A3ᵛ; II: A2, A2ᵛ, A4; III: A3, A3ᵛ, A4; IV: A3ᵛ, A4, A5ᵛ; V: A2, A4ᵛ, B1, B2, B3ᵛ, B4, C1ᵛ.
Cotignola (Codignola in text), town in Emilia-Romagna, II: A2ᵛ.
Creation (of World), V: A2ᵛ.

Dancing, V: C3ᵛ.
Diligence, I: A3ᵛ.
Doctors of Law and Medicine, in Ferrara, II: A4.
Duomo of Ferrara (Cathedral of Saints George and Maurelius), I: A3, A3ᵛ; II: A4ᵛ; V: A2ᵛ, A3, B2, B3, C3ᵛ, C4.

Emblematics, I: A3ᵛ–A4.
Este, Lucrezia d', duchess of Urbino, I: A3; V: C4.
Este, Marfisa d', III: A4ᵛ.
Eternity, I: A4.
Eve, Old Testament character, V: C1ᵛ.

Faenza, Treaty of, between Pope Clement VIII and Cesare d'Este, I: A2–A2ᵛ.
Fano, town in the duchy of Urbino, II: A2ᵛ.
Fernández de Velasco, Juan, Constable of Castile and León, Spanish governor of Milan 1595–1600, V: B1, B2, B3, B3ᵛ.
Felicity, I: A4.
Ferrante II Gonzaga, prince, later duke, of Guastalla 1575–1630, III: A3ᵛ, A4ᵛ.
Ferrara, deposed duke of, see Cesare d'Este; deposed duchess, see Medici, Virginia dei.
Fireworks and Illuminations, II: A2, A2ᵛ; V: C3ᵛ.
Florence, Cardinal of, see Medici, Alessandro dei.
Foligno, town in Umbria, II: A2.
Fontana, Giovanni, bishop of Ferrara, I: A2ᵛ, A3ᵛ; II: A4.
Fountains, flowing with wine, I: A1ᵛ, A2, A2ᵛ.
Francesco Maria II Della Rovere, duke of Urbino 1574–1621 and 1623–1624, II: A2ᵛ.

Gabrieli, Ottaviano, publisher of Mocante's account, V: A1ᵛ.
Garfignana (Graffignana in text), district in Tuscany, I: A2.
Gattemalata (Erasmo da Maini), condottiere, ca. 1370–1443, II: A2.

Genesis, Biblical Book of, V: A2ᵛ.
Genoa, C4.
George, Saint, V: A3.
George, Saint, V: A3, A3ᵛ.
Giara, Strada della, street in Ferrara, II: A4.
Giudecca, today's Giovecca, street in Ferrara, II: A4ᵛ; V: C3ᵛ.
Giuditta e Oloferne (*Iuditta* in text), Jesuit morality play, V: C3ᵛ.
Giudice, chief civic official of Ferrara, see Rondinelli, Camillo.
Gloria, I: A3ᵛ.
Gloria Aldobrandina, II: A4ᵛ.
Golden Rose, see *Rosa d'Oro.*
Grandees of Spain, in ceremonial functions, V: B3ᵛ, B4ᵛ, C2.
Guastalla, town on the Po, IV: A2ᵛ.
Guilds, in Ferrara (*Arti*), I: A2ᵛ.

Habsburg, as family name, see Austria.
Hackney Horse (*chinea*), bearer of the Host, II: A3, A4.
Henry IV, king of France 1589–1610, II: A2ᵛ.
History, I: A4.
Honor, I: A3ᵛ, A4.
Host, Consecrated (*Corpus Domini*), II: A1ᵛ, A2ᵛ, A3, A4; V: B4, C2ᵛ.
Hymen, god of marriage, V: A3ᵛ.

Indulgences, Special, II: A3, A3ᵛ; V: C3ᵛ.
Infanta, see Isabel of Austria.
Inscriptions, Latin, I: A4; II: A1v, A2, A2ᵛ, A4, A4ᵛ; V: A3ᵛ–A4, B1ᵛ.
Isaac, Old Testament character, V: C1ᵛ.
Isabel of Austria, 1566–1633, Infanta of Spain, bride of Albert of Austria, co-sovereign of the southern Low Countries 1599–1621, V: A3ᵛ, A4, C2ᵛ.
Isola, Este country house north of Ferrara, IV: A3; V: A4, A4ᵛ, B1.

Jacob, Old Testament character, V: C1ᵛ.
Jesuits, in Ferrara, V: C3ᵛ.
Jews, in Ferrara, I: A3ᵛ.
John XIII, pope 965–972, II: A2.
Joseph, Old Testament character, V: A2ᵛ.
Judith and Holofernes, Jesuit morality play in Latin, V: C3ᵛ.
Julius II, pope 1502–1513, V: B4.
Justice, I: A3ᵛ.

Keys, of St. Peter, V: A3ᵛ.
Keys, to the Castle of Ferrara, I: A2ᵛ; II: A4ᵛ; to the city of Ferrara, I: A2ᵛ; II: A4.

Loreto, town in the Marches, II: A2.
Lugo, town in Emilia-Romagna, II: A2ᵛ.

Macerata, town in the Marches, II: A2.
Mantua, city and duchy in Lombardy, II: A3.

Mantua, duke of in 1598, see Vincenzo I Gonzaga.

Margaret of Austria, queen of Spain 1599–1612, V: throughout.

Masking, V: C3ᵛ.

Massa, town on the Po, IV: A2ᵛ.

Masses and Other Religious Rites or Ceremonies, I: A3, A3ᵛ; II: A1ᵛ, A2, A2ᵛ, A3, A3ᵛ, A4ᵛ; V: A3, B2ᵛ, B3–C3ᵛ, C4.

Maurelius, Saint, patron of Ferrara, II: A3, A3ᵛ; V: A3.

Maurelius, Saint, V: A3.

Medici, Alessandro dei, cardinal, V: A4, B1ᵛ, B4, C3, C3ᵛ.

Medici, Virginia dei, consort of Cesare d'Este and duchess of Modena and Reggio, I: A2.

Milan, V: C4.

Military Displays, IV: A2ᵛ, A3.

Mocante, Giovan Paolo, papal master of ceremonies and author of the account of the queen's visit, V: A1ᵛ.

Modena and Reggio, duke of in 1598, see Cesare d'Este; duchess of, see Medici, Virginia dei.

Montagna Grande, Porta and Strada della, gate and street in Ferrara, II: A4ᵛ.

Moses, Old Testament character, V: A2ᵛ.

Muses, I: A4.

Music and Musicians, I: A2ᵛ; II: A3, A3ᵛ, A4; III: A3; IV: A3ᵛ; V: A3, B2, B2ᵛ, B3, B4–B4ᵛ, C1, C1ᵛ–C4.

Narni, town in Umbria, II: A1ᵛ.

Nerva, M. Cocceis, Roman emperor A.D. 96–98, II: A2.

Oratory and Public Prayers, II: A4; III: A2ᵛ; V: B2–B2ᵛ, C1ᵛ–C2.

Ostiglia (Ostia in text), town on the Po in the duchy of Mantua, IV: A2ᵛ.

Pages, see Young Patricians in Costume.

Painting, personification, I: A4.

Paintings, in festival *apparati*, I: A4; II: A4ᵛ; V: A3ᵛ, A4.

Palazzo Ducale or Communale, on the site of today's Palazzo del Municipio in Ferrara, and then connected to the Castello Estense, I: A2; II: A4; IV: A4; V: A2–A2ᵛ, A3ᵛ.

Paul, Saint, I: A3ᵛ, A4; II: A4ᵛ; V: A2.

Peace, I: A3ᵛ.

Perosso, Guido, papal master of ceremonies, V: B2, B2ᵛ.

Pesaro, town in the duchy of Urbino, II: A2ᵛ.

Peter, Saint, I: A3ᵛ; II: A4ᵛ; V: A2ᵛ.

Phaeton, Sisters of (periphrasis for poplar trees), II: A4.

Philip III, king of Spain 1598–1621, V: A2, A3ᵛ, A4, B4ᵛ–C2, C2ᵛ.

Piediluca, Cascata di, site in Umbria near Narni, II: A2.

Po River, III: A2ᵛ; IV: A2–A3.

Po, river god, II: A4.

Polymnia, muse of Sublime Hymn, I: A4.

Ponte Aucura, landing place on the Po near Ferrara, III: A2ᵛ.

Pontelagoscuro, landing place on the Po north of Ferrara, IV: A3.

Indexes

Theatrical Production, V: C3ᵛ.
Tobias, character in apocryphal Book of Tobias, V: C2.
Trajan's Column, monument in Rome, II: A4ᵛ.
Treaty Between Clement VIII and Cesare d'Este, see Faenza, Treaty of.
Triumphal Arches, I: A2ᵛ, A3ᵛ–A4; II: A1ᵛ, A2, A2ᵛ, A4ᵛ; V: A3ᵛ–A4, B2.
Trojan War, I: A2.

Urbino, duchess of in 1598, see Este, Lucrezia d'.
Urbino, duke of in 1598, see Francesco Maria II Della Rovere.

Venetian Ambassadors, special delegation sent to call upon Pope Clement VIII,
    III: A2–A2ᵛ.
Venice, II: A3; IV: A2ᵛ.
Vincenzo I Gonzaga, duke of Mantua 1587–1612, III: A2ᵛ–A4ᵛ; IV: A2ᵛ.
Virtue, I: A4.

Young Patricians in Costume, sent as a delegation to greet and serve state guests
    of the city, I: A2ᵛ, A3ᵛ; II: A2, A2ᵛ, A4.

Like other volumes in the Renaissance Triumphs and Magnificences series, **1598: A Year of Pageantry in Late Renaissance Ferrara** is a facsimile edition of Renaissance festival accounts with a critical introduction. Unlike previous volumes in the series, which deal with a single festive event and reproduce one principal document, this one covers six triumphal entries and reproduces five different printed accounts, along with several separate engravings. The various events stretch over a period of ten months and have a number of different protagonists, but they are united in that they all relate to the devolution of the duchy of Ferrara to the States of the Church and the ensuing state visit by Pope Clement VIII.

The first purpose of this volume is to make rare primary sources available to scholars in the disciplines of art history, political and social history, and literary and theater history. The long critical introduction provides pertinent background information in political history, the history of pageantry, and the history of the printed festival account, or *livret*, and interprets the most striking iconographical and literary elements of the festivals.

Bonner Mitchell is Professor of French and Italian at the University of Missouri-Columbia. His many publications include *A Renaissance Entertainment: Festivities for the Wedding of the Duke of Florence, 1539* (Columbia: Univ. of Missouri Press, 1968); *Rome in the High Renaissance: The Age of Leo X* (Norman: Univ. of Oklahoma Press, 1973); *Italian Civic Pageantry in the High Renaissance: A Descriptive Bibliography of Triumphal Entries . . .* (Florence: Leo S. Olschki, 1979); and *The Majesty of the State: Triumphal Progresses of Foreign Sovereigns in Renaissance Italy* (Florence: Olschki, 1986), as well as numerous articles.

mRts

medieval & Renaissance texts & studies
is the publishing program of the
Center for Medieval and Early Renaissance Studies
at the State University of New York at Binghamton.

mRts emphasizes books that are needed —
texts, translations, and major research tools.

mRts aims to publish the highest quality scholarship
in attractive and durable format at modest cost.